THE FOUR NOBLE TRUTHS

THE FOUNDATION OF BUDDHIST THOUGHT SERIES

The Four Noble Truths

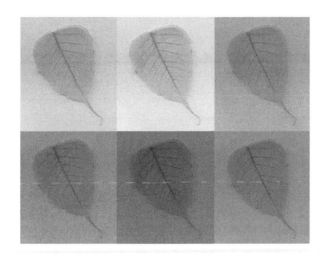

VOLUME I

GESHE TASHI TSERING

FOREWORD BY LAMA ZOPA RINPOCHE

EDITED BY GORDON MCDOUGALL

Wisdom

Wisdom Publications
199 Elm Street
Somerville, MA 02144 USA
www.wisdomexperience.org

Library of Congress Cataloging-in-Publication Data
Tashi Tsering, Geshe, 1958–
  The four noble truths / Geshe Tashi Tsering ; edited by Gordon Mcdougall.—1st ed.
      p. cm.—(Foundation of Buddhist thought ; vol. 1)
  Includes bibliographical references and index.
  ISBN 0-86171-270-6 (pbk. : alk. paper)
  1. Four Noble Truths. I. Mcdougall, Gordon, 1948– II. Title. III. Series.
  BQ4230.T37 2005
  294.3'42—dc22

                           2004031062

ISBN 978-0-86171-270-0   EBOOK ISBN 978-0-86171-964-8

24 23 22 21
7 6

Cover and interior design by Gopa&Ted2, Inc. Set in Goudy 10.5/16 pt. Author photo by Robin Bath.

Wisdom Publications' books are printed on acid-free paper and meet the guidelines for permanence and durability set by the Committee on Production Guidelines for Book Longevity of the Council on Library Resources.

Printed in the United States of America.

Please visit fscus.org.

Contents

FOREWORD

THE BUDDHA'S MESSAGE is a universal one. We all search for happiness but somehow fail to find it because we are looking for it in the wrong way. Only when we start cherishing others will true happiness grow within us. And so the Buddha's essential teaching is one of compassion and ethics, combined with the wisdom that understands the nature of reality. The teachings of the Buddha contain everything needed to eliminate suffering and make life truly meaningful, and as such the teachings are not only relevant to today's world, but vital.

This is the message my precious teacher, Lama Thubten Yeshe, gave to his Western students. His vision to present the Dharma in a way that is accessible and relevant to everyone continues and grows. His organization, the Foundation for the Preservation of the Mahayana Tradition (FPMT), now has centers all over the world, and Lama's work is carried on by many of his students.

The Foundation of Buddhist Thought, developed by Geshe Tashi Tsering, is one of the core courses of the FPMT's integrated education program. The essence of Tibetan Buddhism can be found within its six subjects. The Foundation of Buddhist Thought serves as a wonderful basis for further study in Buddhism, as well as a tool to transform our everyday lives.

Geshe Tashi has been the resident teacher at Jamyang Buddhist

Centre, London, since 1994. He has been very beneficial in guiding the students there and in many other centers where he teaches. Besides his profound knowledge—he is a Lharampa Geshe, the highest educational qualification within our tradition—his excellent English and his deep understanding of his Western students means that he can present the Dharma in a way that is both accessible and relevant. His wisdom, compassion, and humor are combined with a genuine gift as a teacher. You will see within the six books of the Foundation of Buddhist Thought series the same combination of profound understanding and heart advice that can guide beginner and experienced practitioners alike on the spiritual path.

Whether you read this book out of curiosity or as part of your spiritual journey, I sincerely hope that you find it beneficial and that it shows you a way to open your heart and develop your wisdom.

Lama Zopa Rinpoche
Spiritual Director
The Foundation for the Preservation of the Mahayana Tradition

Preface

THE TIBETAN BUDDHIST monastery I trained in, Sera, lies outside the city of Mysore in South India. It was built by refugees from the original Sera Monastery near the capital of Tibet who had escaped following the Chinese Communist occupation in 1959. The Sera I joined in 1970 as a thirteen-year-old monk is now unrecognizable—its small cluster of buildings has now expanded to become a sprawling campus. At that time, there was only one mail delivery a week—sometimes only one every two weeks. These days young monks have laptops to exchange emails whenever they want or else they can go to one of four or five crowded internet cafés.

It is not only the physical monastery that has changed. The worldview of the monks is different as well. When I was studying Buddhist philosophy, very few monks had any doubt about the accuracy of the cosmology in the traditional *Abhidharma* texts, which give precise dimensions for the universe; the vast majority believed that the structure and origin of the universe was exactly as the texts explained. Although a few elder monks still take the texts literally, nowadays most of the monks have either seen the outside world or have at least seen science documentaries. Whether their understanding of modern science is good or not, they no longer accept the *Abhidharma* explanation of the universe literally.

Such radical changes at one small Buddhist monastery in India in such a short span of time mirror changes in the rest of the world. Huge technological, economic, and scientific developments have transformed both humanity and the planet we live in. In many cases the changes have been positive, but certain changes have been negative and even extremely destructive.

And although technological advances have solved many superficial difficulties that humanity once faced, the fundamental human problems remain as they always have. In both wealthy and developing countries, we find the same basic human difficulties, whether dissatisfaction or disharmony, poverty or prejudice, and see that, as always, they are mainly created by human beings themselves.

In this world so radically changed yet still grappling with the same fundamental concerns, I feel great benefit can be gained from reexamining the old wisdom. For this reason I chose to write this series of books.

The people now interested in studying and practicing Buddhism live in the twenty-first century, in the middle of all this modern technological and economic development. Their leisure, lifestyle, and commitments are totally different from the norm of even just fifty or sixty years ago. I feel, therefore, that Buddhist texts and study materials must take into account modern society's lifestyle.

Furthermore, due to the ease of travel, many Westerners have received teachings in Asia or have heard Asian teachers in the West. For many students of Buddhism, study has been in a piecemeal fashion, dependent upon whatever teachings were available. Many people have listened to various subjects but have never received a solid overview, one starting from a fundamental Buddhist teaching, such as the four noble truths, and progressing systematically up to the most profound teachings, such as those of highest yoga tantra. For that kind of person, I wanted to provide a structured program.

And I wanted to make it as accessible and relevant as possible. Today vastly more books on Buddhism are available than even ten or fifteen years ago, but many are either translations of great texts and therefore quite traditional in style, or else they are written by Western scholars and hence academic and dense. Both kinds of books can benefit people, but often they are not so accessible. For a long time I have felt that there is a need for Buddhist teachings explained in some detail but in very plain language, without Buddhist jargon. No question the Buddha's teachings are relevant, but the way they are presented makes a great difference as to whether people can actually assimilate them into their everyday lives. It is my hope that this series provides something easily readable, yet still with depth and structure, that allows people to read and study over a year or two and take these wonderful teachings into their lives in a way that is truly meaningful. That has been my goal for The Foundation of Buddhist Thought series.

I have chosen six subjects with the hope that they will lay out a comprehensive overview of Buddhist thought. The four noble truths, the first teaching the Buddha gave after he attained enlightenment, is the logical starting point. His Holiness the Dalai Lama, who has given teachings on the four noble truths on many occasions, says that they are the blueprint for all Buddhist teaching and practice. Within them lie the root of all Buddhist philosophy and the entire path to enlightenment. Whatever we study after the four noble truths will echo back to this most essential teaching, and conversely this teaching will be revealed in everything else we study.

If the four noble truths explain the human condition, the next two books, *Relative Truth, Ultimate Truth* and *Buddhist Psychology,* deal with the Buddhist theories of reality, external as well as internal. Then based on these, the remaining three volumes address what it means to be a practicing Mahayana Buddhist. Volume 4 looks at the vast altruistic mind called the mind of enlightenment *(bodhichitta)*, and volume 5 looks at the wisdom that understands that all things are interdependent and lack intrinsic nature. The final volume gives a glimpse into how the tantric practices are done.

These books evolved from the two-year courses I have been leading in Great Britain, France, and Spain since 1997, as well as from the correspondence course that grew out of the campus courses. If you find the books beneficial, you might consider enrolling in The Foundation of Buddhist Thought correspondence course, where you will explore the subjects in more depth under the guidance of qualified tutors.

If we examine our lives, it is not difficult to see how we are continuously searching for some form of happiness and trying to avoid the pitfalls and dissatisfaction that seem to plague our existence. This is as true for us living in this modern technological world as it was for the people of the Buddha's time. And now, just as then, we are continually getting it wrong. Everything the Buddha taught was to lead us out of the suffering we so unskillfully inflict on ourselves and to bring us to a profound and lasting happiness. The problem is not one of relevance but of accessibility. I hope that this series will allow you to enter into one of the world's great philosophical traditions.

Geshe Tashi Tsering

Editor's Preface

The Four Noble Truths is the end product of a long and very dynamic process. It is a modified version of the course book written by Geshe Tashi Tsering for the first module of his study program, The Foundation of Buddhist Thought.

In 1994, when Geshe Tashi took up his role of resident teacher at Jamyang Buddhist Centre in London, he saw that the text-based, passive learning usually associated with Tibetan Buddhism in Western Dharma centers often failed to connect with the material in a meaningful way, and so, incorporating Western pedagogic methods, he devised a two-year, six-module course that he felt would give a solid overview of Buddhist thought.

The sources for this series from Wisdom Publications, of which this is the first volume, are the transcripts of Geshe Tashi's teachings from the first two London courses. Geshe Tashi reworked these texts into the materials you have in your hands. Most of Tibetan philosophical literature is derived from oral teachings, and this is true to some extent of each of the books in this series, but I also think that these texts surpass this level. Well-read in Western science and philosophy, and with a good command of English, Geshe Tashi is very much the author—in every sense of the word—of these books.

When I first met him in 1992, Geshe-la was staying at Nalanda

Monastery in southern France, studying both the English language and the Western mind. My respect for the diligence and enthusiasm with which he worked has only increased over the years. At the time, however, I had no idea of the depth of his knowledge.

Born in 1958, in Purang, Tibet, Geshe Tashi escaped to India with his parents a year later. He entered Sera Mey Monastic University at thirteen, and spent the next sixteen years working for his Geshe degree, graduating as a Lharampa Geshe, the highest possible level. He is a classmate of another notable Geshe who is also very important to Buddhism in the West, Geshe Thupten Jinpa, chief English language translator of His Holiness the Dalai Lama.

After a year at the Highest Tantric College (Gyuto), Geshe-la began his teaching career in Kopan Monastery in Kathmandu, the principal monastery of the Foundation for the Preservation of the Mahayana Tradition (FPMT). Geshe Tashi then moved to the Gandhi Foundation College in Nagpur, and it was at that time that the FPMT's Spiritual Director, Lama Thubten Zopa Rinpoche, asked him to teach in the West. After two years at Nalanda Monastery in France, in 1994 Geshe Tashi became the resident teacher at Jamyang Buddhist Centre in London.

His first years at Jamyang set the tone for his residency. When the center moved to a derelict courthouse in 1996, Geshe Tashi worked alongside the volunteers—scraping walls, clearing debris—I even saw him in overalls and wellington boots clearing out blocked drains. He has been very much part of the Jamyang community ever since.

And it is this sense of Western ease combined with his deep insight into Buddhist philosophy that has informed his teaching. Geshe Tashi not only understands us, but also in many ways is one of us and so can offer Eastern wisdom with a Western approach—one that we are comfortable with and one that is also utterly relevant to our lives. The Gelug school is thought to be the most scholastic of the four traditions in Tibetan Buddhism, and if you engage Geshe-la in debate you will certainly feel the sharpness of his intellect. However, his emphasis is always on the experiential—according to Geshe Tashi, if it stays academic, it is worthless. Comfort might be found in dry scholasticism while the heart remains untouched, but this is a comfort he never allows us.

As with the other books in the series, many people have been involved with its development. I would particularly like to thank Bhikku Bodhi for allowing us to use his translation of the sutra, the core of this book.

I would also like to offer my warmest thanks to Lama Zopa Rinpoche, the head of the FPMT and the inspiration for the group of study programs to which The Foundation of Buddhist Thought belongs. Rinpoche is the font from which all else flows.

There are too many other people who have been involved with the course and the books to mention by name, but I would like to sincerely thank them all—those who helped to develop the course; the transcribers, readers, and designers of the books; and the tutors of the course among them. And of course, Geshe Tashi, an amazing inspiration.

It has been a real joy to edit Geshe Tashi's words. My very limited knowledge has undoubtedly meant that his ideas have been blurred and distorted in some instances, and for this I offer my deepest apologies. It is my sincere hope that the reader will gain the same inspiration and insight from this book that has been gained by the many hundreds of students who have already been fortunate enough to study The Foundation of Buddhist Thought.

Gordon McDougall

❧ The Four Noble Truths Sutra

OVER 2,500 YEARS AGO the historical Buddha, Shakyamuni, became enlightened. Having forsaken a life of luxury as the prince Siddhartha and endured six years as an ascetic, suffering deliberate deprivation in his search for the truth, he realized that in neither extreme was truth to be found. Only then, sitting under the Bodhi tree by the river Neranjara, did he overcome the last of his inner demons and break through to the truth of his existence, finally reaching the cessation of his human suffering. He became the Buddha, the Awakened One.

At first he remained silent, but then, after forty-nine days, he journeyed from Bodhgaya to Sarnath, a small town near the sacred city of Varanasi in central India. Here, he met his five former companions, the ascetics with whom he had shared his six years of hardship. At first they were suspicious, thinking he had renounced the search for truth, but upon seeing his radiance, they begged him for teachings. Thereupon the Buddha explained to them the four noble truths, and it is these four truths that comprise the sutra below and the core subject of this book.

Only after the Buddha's passing did his disciples, now vast in number, come together to try to preserve his precious teachings. The sutras we have now in the Buddhist canon come from actual discourses of the Buddha that were memorized by the Buddha's disciples and passed down in an oral lineage. Only centuries later were they written down, retaining much of the convention of the oral tradition. The repetition of phrases and even paragraphs was designed for easy memorization, and the whole style was developed to facilitate ritual recitation. As such sutras can be difficult reading, but their content, the actual words of the Buddha, are an infallible map out of the suffering that currently traps us.

The following sutra—one of the most famous—records the Buddha's very first teaching, *Setting the Wheel of Dharma in Motion*. It is also called the *First Turning of the Wheel of Dharma* or, more simply, the *Four Noble Truths Sutra*, because the four noble truths comprise its essence.

Thus have I heard.

On one occasion the Blessed One was dwelling at Varanasi in the Deer Park at Isipatana. There the Blessed One addressed the bhikkhus of the group of five thus:

"Bhikkhus, these two extremes should not be followed by one who has gone forth into homelessness. What two? The pursuit of sensual happiness in sensual pleasures, which is low, vulgar, the way of worldlings, ignoble, unbeneficial; and the pursuit of self-mortification, which is painful, ignoble, unbeneficial. Without veering toward either of these extremes, the Tathagata has awakened to the middle way, which gives rise to vision, which gives rise to knowledge, which leads to peace, to direct knowledge, to enlightenment, to nibbana. And what, bhikkhus, is that middle way awakened to by the Tathagata, which gives rise to vision…which leads to nibbana? It is this noble eightfold path; that is, right view, right intention, right speech, right action, right livelihood, right effort, right mindfulness, right concentration. This, bhikkhus, is that middle way awakened to by the Tathagata, which gives rise to vision, which gives rise to knowledge, which leads to peace, to direct knowledge, to enlightenment, to nibbana.

"Now this, bhikkhus, is the noble truth of suffering: birth is suffering, aging is suffering, illness is suffering, death is suffering; union with what is displeasing is suffering; separation from what is pleasing is suffering; not to get what one wants is suffering; in brief, the five aggregates subject to clinging are suffering.

"Now this, bhikkhus, is the noble truth of the origin of suffering: it is this craving that leads to renewed existence, accompanied by delight and lust, seeking delight here and there; that is, craving for sensual pleasures, craving for existence, craving for extermination.

"Now this, bhikkhus, is the noble truth of the cessation of suffering: it is the remainderless fading away and cessation of that same craving, the giving up and relinquishing of it, freedom from it, non-reliance on it.

"Now this, bhikkhus, is the noble truth of the way leading to the cessation of suffering: it is this noble eightfold path; that is, right view, right intention, right speech, right action, right livelihood, right effort, right mindfulness, right concentration.

"'This is the noble truth of suffering': thus, bhikkhus, in regard to things unheard before, there arose in me vision, knowledge, wisdom, true knowledge, and light.

"'This noble truth of suffering is to be fully understood': thus, bhikkhus, in regard to things unheard before, there arose in me vision, knowledge, wisdom, true knowledge, and light.

"'This noble truth of suffering has been fully understood': thus, bhikkhus, in regard to things unheard before, there arose in me vision, knowledge, wisdom, true knowledge, and light.

"'This is the noble truth of the origin of suffering': thus, bhikkhus, in regard to things unheard before, there arose in me vision, knowledge, wisdom, true knowledge, and light.

"'This noble truth of the origin of suffering is to be abandoned': thus, bhikkhus, in regard to things unheard before, there arose in me vision, knowledge, wisdom, true knowledge, and light.

"'This noble truth of the origin of suffering has been abandoned': thus, bhikkhus, in regard to things unheard before, there arose in me vision, knowledge, wisdom, true knowledge, and light.

"'This is the noble truth of the cessation of suffering': thus, bhikkhus, in regard to things unheard before, there arose in me vision, knowledge, wisdom, true knowledge, and light.

"'This noble truth of the cessation of suffering is to be realized': thus, bhikkhus, in regard to things unheard before, there arose in me vision, knowledge, wisdom, true knowledge, and light.

"'This noble truth of the cessation of suffering has been realized': thus, bhikkhus, in regard to things unheard before, there arose in me vision, knowledge, wisdom, true knowledge, and light.

"'This is the noble truth of the way leading to the cessation of suffering': thus, bhikkhus, in regard to things unheard before, there arose in me vision, knowledge, wisdom, true knowledge, and light.

"'This noble truth of the way leading to the cessation of suffering is to be developed': thus, bhikkhus, in regard to things unheard before, there arose in me vision, knowledge, wisdom, true knowledge, and light.

"'This noble truth of the way leading to the cessation of suffering has been developed': thus, bhikkhus, in regard to things unheard before, there arose in me vision, knowledge, wisdom, true knowledge, and light.

"So long, bhikkhus, as my knowledge and vision of these four noble truths as they really are in their three phases and twelve aspects was not thoroughly purified in this way, I did not claim to have wakened to the unsurpassed perfect enlightenment in this world with its devas, Mara, and Brahma, in this generation with its ascetics and brahmins, its devas and humans. But when my knowledge and vision of these four noble truths as they really are in their three phases and twelve aspects was thoroughly purified in this way, then I claimed to have awakened to the unsurpassed perfect enlightenment in this world with its devas, Mara, and Brahma, in this generation with its ascetics and brahmins, its devas and humans. The knowledge and vision arose in me: 'Unshakable is the liberation of my mind. This is my last birth. Now there is no more renewed existence.'"

This is what the Blessed One said.[1]

1 SETTING THE WHEEL OF DHARMA IN MOTION

The Four Truths

I HAVE BEEN A BUDDHIST all my life. My childhood, my monastic schooling, and now my work have all been steeped in the teachings of the Buddha. While I have questioned many philosophical points within my training—debate being a significant element of Tibetan Buddhist education—I have never questioned the essential message of the Buddha or wondered whether it was still relevant.

Since coming to the West and teaching students who demand logical explanations for the most basic Buddhist concepts, I have had to reassess my own core beliefs. But the more I see Western students integrating Buddhist principles and practices into their lives, the more I understand just how universal the Buddha's message is. Although you will doubtless come across many foreign terms and concepts in this book, everything the Buddha taught has the power to go straight to your heart. My job is to make sure what you read is meaningful and intelligible so you can fully appreciate its relevance.

The *Four Noble Truths Sutra* is the Buddha's first and most essential teaching. It contains the framework of all the many discourses he gave during his forty-year teaching career. If the language and style hinder the clear understanding of his meaning, then hopefully, by the time you have finished this book, you will have a much better grasp of this all-important sutra.

In Tibetan monasteries, as in most traditions within Mahayana Buddhism, the *sutras* (the discourses of the Buddha) and the *shastras* (the canonical commentaries) that are studied originate from the Sanskrit-language canon. In this case, however, we are using the sutra translated from the Pali language. Although it differs slightly in style and structure from the Sanskrit, the differences are minor, and in the West this is the better-known version.

The four noble truths are:

1. The noble truth of suffering
2. The noble truth of the origin of suffering
3. The noble truth of the cessation of suffering and the origin of suffering
4. The noble truth of the path that leads to the cessation of suffering and the origin of suffering

The first two noble truths, the noble truths of suffering and of the origin of suffering, really reflect the nature of our present life—they function continually within each of us. The truth of cessation and the truth of the path that leads to cessation are the methods to eliminate suffering and its origin. We need to cultivate them within ourselves in order to overcome our difficulties. Thus, these four noble truths show us not only the nature of our present life in its entirety, but also the possibility of moving beyond this very limited existence into an existence that is free from suffering and its origin.

The first noble truth, the noble truth of suffering (*dukkha* in Pali), refers to the pain, distress, suffering, anxiety, and dissatisfaction that physically and particularly mentally exist within us. After teaching the first noble truth, the Buddha then explains that the cause of suffering— the second noble truth—is craving, desire, and attachment. With the third noble truth the Buddha shows that there is a means by which suffering can be eradicated forever, and through the fourth noble truth he demonstrates the way to do this. The path that the Buddha lays out to enable us to achieve this eradication of suffering is called the *noble eightfold path*, which we discuss in chapter 5. Within the four truths we find two distinct sets of cause and result. Suffering is a result and the origin of suffering is its cause. Similarly, the truth of cessation, or peace, is a result, and the path that leads to cessation is its cause.

The four noble truths lay down the blueprint for the entire body of the Buddha's thought and practice and set up the basic framework of the individual's path to enlightenment. They encapsulate all of Buddhist philosophy. Therefore studying, meditating, and fully understanding this teaching is very important, because without an understanding of the four noble truths it is impossible to fully integrate the concepts and practices of Buddhism into our daily lives.

We all have an instinctive wish to have happiness and avoid suffering. This feeling does not arise as a result of training, education, or culture; it is innate. The teaching on the four noble truths presents an effective means to achieving this end. The suffering we want to overcome does not come from nowhere. It arises from its own particular causes and conditions. In this teaching the Buddha details the suffering that we experience in everyday life, from the very coarse forms of suffering to the very subtle forms of which we are not even consciously aware. He also explains the causes of that suffering with equal precision.

Similarly, the happiness that we all want does not come from nowhere but arises from its own causes and conditions. Happiness in this case has nothing to do with temporary sense pleasures but refers to the higher states of happiness—the happiness that remains unaffected despite changing external circumstances. Although the cessation of suffering is not in itself a feeling, achieving that kind of cessation through the right path is the highest form of happiness. The path that will lead to the fulfillment of our most basic aspiration to overcome suffering and achieve happiness is explained in this teaching very clearly.

The two main Buddhist traditions, Theravada and Mahayana, have different sets of scriptures. The Theravada is an earlier tradition whose teachings are recorded in the Pali texts, while the Mahayana is based on Sanskrit texts that were written down later. The countries that follow the Theravada tradition strongly emphasize reading, reciting, and learning the actual discourses of the Buddha. In the Tibetan monasteries, which follow the Mahayana tradition, we study the four noble truths on many occasions over the course of our education, but we do not typically study the sutra itself. Usually we study this topic in conjunction with the teachings that emphasize the bodhisattva aspiration for enlightenment for the sake of all other beings. For example, one of the main texts that we study in the monastery is Maitreya's *Ornament of Clear Realization (Abhisamayalamkara)*, and the main topic of that text is the way bodhisattvas train their minds on the path. The four noble truths is a key subject in illustrating this training. Similarly, in the Mahayana, the noble eightfold path is taught only implicitly within the teachings on the bodhisattva conduct rather than laid out explicitly.

In Tibetan monasteries, study of the four noble truths is combined with the examination of what we call the sixteen characteristics of the four noble truths. Each noble truth is explained, studied, and meditated on by focusing on four defining characteristics. For instance, the first noble truth, the noble truth of suffering, is studied by analyzing its four characteristics of impermanence, suffering, selflessness, and emptiness.

Although the sutra is the main source of all of this, in the Tibetan system the main focus of our study on the four noble truths is the commentaries, which include extensive and elaborate explanations about each of the truths.

THE STRUCTURE OF THE SUTRA

As you can see from the *Four Noble Truths Sutra*, the Buddha describes each noble truth in a slightly different way. He says that the first noble truth should be understood, the second noble truth should be abandoned, the third noble truth should be realized, and the last noble truth should be developed. This indicates that although the four noble truths are one subject, the way we study and meditate on each truth differs slightly.

The Buddha says that we must *understand* the truth of suffering. We will overcome suffering eventually as we practice the other noble truths, but first we must understand what suffering is. This is logical. Before taking medicine, we must understand our illness, before abandoning suffering, we need to really understand it. Therefore, at this stage, understanding the truth of suffering is the most important thing we can do, and this requires a clear recognition of its importance and a systematic study of the steps we must take to complete our task.

The Buddha says that the second noble truth, the truth of origin, should be *abandoned*. So here we have to diligently search for the best method to totally abandon the origin of suffering. This requires a different way of studying and meditating. The truth of cessation, on the other hand, should be realized or attained. Therefore, to begin, we must definitely come to understand that this can be achieved and that we ourselves are capable of achieving it. And naturally we now come to the fourth noble truth, the truth of the path, which we need to develop in order to overcome suffering.

In the first section of the sutra the Buddha very clearly presents the task ahead of us. In the next section he repeats each noble truth three times, each time with a slightly different emphasis and a slightly different flavor. This repetition represents the three phases of understanding that the Buddha himself acquired in his ever-deepening realization of these four truths. The three phases are as follows: knowing the nature of the truth, knowing what needs to be done in connection with that truth, and finally accomplishing what needs to be done.

In regard to the noble truth of suffering, in the first phase the Buddha explains what suffering is, and in the second phase he explains that this suffering should be understood. Then, in the final phase of realizing this noble truth, he explains complete attainment—the fact that when someone has understood suffering fully and completely, this is all that needs to be accomplished.

It is the same with the other noble truths. In relation to the origin of suffering, the Buddha explains what it is, that it needs to be abandoned, and that once abandoned, there is a state of complete attainment and suffering can never return. For the cessation of suffering, the Buddha again explains what it is, that it needs to be realized, and that once it is realized, that is the final point, which can never reverse into noncessation. In fact, this point is liberation or enlightenment. Finally, the Buddha presents the truth of the path in the context of the noble eightfold path, explaining that it must be developed, and that once it is developed, there is nothing that remains to be done.

At the end of the sutra, after explaining the three phases of each noble truth, making twelve aspects in all, the Buddha says, "So long, bhikkhus, as my knowledge and vision of these four noble truths as they really are in their three phases and twelve aspects was not thoroughly purified in this way, I did not claim to have awakened to the unsurpassed perfect enlightenment…." Only after each noble truth has been realized in its own unique way is complete attainment possible.

The Order of the Four Noble Truths

The Buddha taught the four noble truths in a very specific order, and this has nothing to do with the order in which things arise in reality. In reality, the cause must naturally come first and be followed by the result; it cannot be the other way around. There is a cause that produces suffering, and there is a path that leads us to the end of suffering. However, in both sets of cause and effect that comprise the four noble truths, the order is reversed—the result of suffering is presented first followed by the cause of the origin of suffering. The second set presents the result of cessation and then the cause of the path.

In his *Great Stages of the Path (Lamrim Chenmo)* the Tibetan master Lama Tsongkhapa explains that despite not following the natural sequence, this is the particular order that the student should be taught because it represents the way each truth is psychologically established within us. For example, when we start to work with the first two noble truths, it is natural that we first realize that there is suffering. That realization will then lead us to search for the causes of that suffering. It is the same with the second set. When we see that there is suffering and that it has an origin, the next step is to ask if there is any way that suffering can cease. In so doing, we establish that cessation is possible, and then we look for methods that can lead to it.

Say, for example, the sink in my apartment is full of cups and pots, but when I turn on the hot water tap to wash them, nothing happens; there is no hot water. Seeing the flashing red light on the boiler, I phone someone to come and fix it. That is the natural process. When we discover a problem, we go back and try to find its origin. When we see the result, naturally we look for the cause, so the result of identifying a problem is a motivation that starts us off toward the solution. Our minds naturally operate in that way, which is why the Buddha taught the four noble truths in this unique sequence. Therefore, for the Buddhist practitioner who wants to pursue the spiritual path, the realization of this particular sequence is psychologically very natural and helpful. Maitreya's *Sublime Continuum (Uttaratantra)* compares these four stages to overcoming an illness.

> Just as disease needs to be diagnosed, its cause eliminated, a healthy state achieved and the remedy implemented, so also should suffering, its causes, its cessation and path be known, removed, attained and undertaken.[2]

It is not until we notice we are sick that we begin to look for the source of our sickness, and seeing that there is a cure, try to obtain it. This is suffering, origin, cessation, and path.

THE ETYMOLOGY OF THE TERM FOUR NOBLE TRUTHS

It may be useful to clarify what a *noble truth* actually is, because *truth* has different meanings in different contexts. In Buddhism there are many truths—the two truths, the four noble truths, and so on—and we need to be very careful and not assume that *truth* always means the same thing.

The modifier *noble* means truth as perceived by *arya* beings, those beings who have had a direct realization of emptiness or selflessness. *Noble* means something seen by arya beings as it really is, and in this case it is four recognitions—suffering, origin, cessation, and path. Arya beings see all types of suffering—physical and mental, gross and subtle—exactly as they are, as suffering. For people like us, who do not have the direct realization of emptiness, although we may understand certain levels of physical and mental experiences as suffering, it is impossible for us to see all the levels of suffering for what they are. Instead we may see some things as desirable when in truth they are suffering. This may sound counterintuitive, but if you examine society it is fairly easy to see what I mean. What most of us chase after thinking it is happiness actually has the potential to bring just the opposite.

It is the same with the other three subjects, all of which are seen by the arya beings as they are, on all levels of subtlety. We ordinary beings cannot see them in the same way because we lack the direct realization of the nature of reality.

The Benefits of Studying the Four Noble Truths

What prompts us to embark upon a spiritual journey? As we first become interested in Buddhism, I think this is a question we need to ask ourselves. His Holiness the Dalai Lama says that our interest in the spiritual life is "something very instinctive and there is no need to prove it is there. Happiness is something that we all aspire to achieve and of course we naturally have a right to fulfill this aspiration."[3]

We should try to understand our deepest motivation clearly from the very beginning and not just accept intellectually that we all want to be happy or because somebody like His Holiness says it, but only as a result of our own thorough investigation. We need to see whether the wish to be happy is instinctive, as His Holiness has said, and if so whether it is always present, fueling our actions. We also need to be aware of how skillfully or unskillfully we are actually fulfilling that need. This examination is our starting point.

The minimum advantage we will gain by studying the four noble truths is that we will develop some confidence that the problems and difficulties in our life can be stopped. At present our life is completely conditioned by factors outside of our control, but by clearly seeing the things that actually cause our problems and that they can

be eliminated, we can determine that there is a remedy for this "conditioned" life. If we can develop confidence in the possibility of cessation—
through reading books, contemplating, and meditating—then I think
we will definitely have good results.

Furthermore, if we see that by following the teachings of the
Buddha we can slowly learn to subdue our minds and finally completely cease our conditioned existence, we will be, in effect, taking
refuge in the Dharma—the Buddha's teachings and the second of the
three refuges. This will naturally lead to a respect for the Buddha himself and then for the Sangha, those realized beings who follow his path,
and so we establish our refuge in the Buddha and the Sangha, the
other two objects of refuge. This will all arise from a thorough ground-
ing in the four noble truths.

The best way to take refuge in the Dharma is to put the path into
practice, and so we go from taking refuge in the Sangha to *becoming*
the Sangha—not necessarily as an ordained monk or nun, but through
the direct realization of emptiness. This is the intermediate benefit of
studying the four noble truths.

Finally, we will come to understand the real nature of our own suffering and see how all beings are exactly the same in this experience,
and so our practice will naturally turn from being primarily concerned
with our own welfare to focusing on the welfare of others. As we
progress, our prejudices and self-interest will fall away, and our activities will become more altruistic. Of course, this can really be achieved
only through understanding and practicing the four noble truths at a
very profound level. The highest benefit of studying the four noble
truths is attaining the mind of enlightenment, or bodhichitta, at
which point we are completely motivated by the wish to free all beings
from suffering and hence work toward our own enlightenment to be
able to do that.

The cessation of suffering is not a gift that someone can give us, but rather it must emerge through our practice of the true path. As we progress, the gap between the uncontrolled, conditioned life we now lead and the core that is pure and perfect peace will narrow. By developing an understanding and then actually practicing the teachings of the four noble truths in our daily lives, we will become greatly beneficial for all other sentient beings, not only helping them bring an end to their suffering but incidentally eliminating our own as well.

The Two Sets of Cause and Effect

One of the key beliefs in Buddhism is that nothing comes into being without a cause, and this law of cause and effect is a fundamental point for understanding the four noble truths. The following table shows two sets of cause and effect: suffering as the result of the origin of suffering and cessation as the result of the path.

	Result	Cause
Problem	1. Suffering	2. Origin
Solution	3. Cessation	4. Path

Although these two sets of cause and effect are very specific, they follow the rule of all causes and effects, and in particular the type of cause and effect called *karma* in Buddhism. *Karma* is an often misunderstood concept. To clarify, natural changes such as planetary rotation or plant growth are not the results of karma. Karma always relates solely to the workings of the mind. Only when there has been some sort of mental action, some sort of intention or volition, does the specific chain reaction of cause and result occur, and thus it is always associated with our mindstate, our feelings or emotions. However, while it is quite easy to see how suffering and its cause are linked with feelings, it may be more difficult to understand this in the context of the second set, cessation and path, as these are more subtle. Nonetheless, cessation and path are also inextricably intertwined.

From a Buddhist perspective, the countless things and events that make up the entire external world, whether associated with our feelings or not, are called *other-powered* because they arise due to other conditions. Nothing comes into being without a cause. In the *Rice Seedling Sutra* the Buddha gives three statements:

> Due to the existence of this, that arises.
> Due to the production of this, that is produced.
> It is thus: due to ignorance there is volition.

The first statement—"due to the existence of this, that arises"—can be applied to all phenomena, permanent and impermanent, and describes interdependent origination. These things exist, then that happens. In Buddhist philosophical terms, for the purpose of meditation, all phenomena are divided into classifications, *permanent* and *impermanent* being a very common division. To briefly describe the difference, *permanent phenomena* are phenomena that do not depend on causes and conditions for their existence. During their existence, there is no moment-to-moment change. In other words, they are static. *Impermanent phenomena* refers to the opposite—things and events that depend on causes and conditions to come into being and that are subject to constant change. Thus *impermanent* in this context means changing moment by moment.

The second statement—"due to the production of this, that is produced"—can be applied only to impermanent phenomena. In order to produce something, the producer must be impermanent, for only impermanent phenomena can produce something that does not already exist. Permanent phenomena cannot. *Permanent* means fixed and unchanging, so how could it go from one state to another, like a seed becoming a flower? Only if something is impermanent, and hence has the potential to change when circumstances and conditions come together, will results and other phenomena arise.

The third statement—"due to ignorance there is volition"—is narrower in scope. Impermanent things do not have the ability to produce any random thing. In order to produce something, the cause must be similar to the result. Ignorance does not produce love—it produces attachment and aversion, and from these the deluded mind creates the wish to act, which is volition.

How the Two Sets Work

The second noble truth is the origin of our suffering. We are ignorant of the fundamental nature of the way things exist, and we feel anxiety because of this. We see things as existing permanently and cling to anything that reinforces our concept of permanence, pushing away anything that threatens it. Attachment and aversion are the roots of all other problems, and they themselves are caused by ignorance. Thus ignorance, attachment, and aversion—what Buddhism calls the *three poisons*—are the origin (the second noble truth) of suffering (the first noble truth).

The relationship in the first set of cause and effect—suffering and its origin—is easy to understand because both truths are impermanent. On one level, the relationship in the the second set—path and cessation—is equally understandable. The path is the practice we do to eliminate our delusions and to increase our positive qualities. This path becomes the final cause of the complete cessation of all our suffering.

But cessation itself is *not* the result of a chain of cause and effect because cessation is permanent, and in order to be either a cause or a result, something must be impermanent. This is a very important point. If something is a result, it means it has come into existence in dependence upon other factors, and so it must, by definition, be impermanent. Permanent phenomena do *not* come into existence due to causes and conditions. They may, however, come into being through other circumstances, such as a state that occurs when various conditions are removed.

This is a little abstract. As I have pointed out, from a Buddhist point of view, a permanent phenomenon means something that never changes and that is never produced by something else. Usually *permanent* describes some sort of state, rather than a physical or mental object with definite causes. Cessation itself is one of the prime examples of a permanent phenomenon, so it may seem strange that we find it here in the second set of cause and result, when in fact it cannot strictly be called a result.

We can use a teacup to illustrate this point. When I pour the tea out, the cup becomes empty. The action of pouring brings a particular result, an empty cup, and by *empty* here I simply mean empty of tea. That lack of tea, however, cannot truly be called a product, because it is an absence, and something cannot produce an absence. Yet there is, nonetheless, a dependent relationship between my pouring action and the cup's empty state.

In the same way, through practicing the path, our suffering gradually decreases, and we finally attain a state that is free from all suffering, ignorance, and the defilements that are the seeds of that suffering. This mere absence of suffering is called *true cessation* and that cessation is a state, not a product. It is not produced by the path; it is not a result per se. As tipping the cup over rids it of tea, following the path rids us of our negativities, and we are left with the state of being free of suffering, which is nirvana.

Nirvana is simply the cessation of suffering, not the annihilation of the person. People often misunderstand this point, thinking that nirvana is the complete cessation of not only suffering but also of the person trying to gain that state. That is not what Buddhist practice is for.

According to Mahayana Buddhism, when suffering and its causes have finally been eliminated, at the time of death the mental and physical aggregates cease, and what is called *cessation without remainder* is achieved. Previously we had achieved nirvana but we had *not* ceased to exist, because throughout our entire practice we had done nothing to stop the continuation of the person. Just as our suffering does not come from external sources but is caused by our own delusions and karma, so the complete end of that suffering arises from the gradual elimination of our delusions. In that way, peace arises from chaos, cessation of suffering arises from suffering, and nirvana arises from samsara.

Nirvana is not out there somewhere in space; it does not drop down from the sky. Cessation will emerge only from our development of wisdom. Buddhahood is an internal state, but because our normal life is focused on the external, there is a very strong tendency to see things such as nirvana or buddhahood as somehow "out there," as physical entities in physical places. That view is mistaken.

Nirvana might seem like a conceptual abstraction, but cessation and the path have very a lot to do with our everyday lives. Although we all want happiness and spend most of the hours of our day trying to get it, most of us are searching in the wrong place entirely. Following the path laid down by the Buddha, as exemplified in the fourth noble truth, we will slowly lessen our suffering, ceasing the delusions as well as their causes, which keep us trapped in conditioned existence.

This is what Buddhism says, but do you agree? You have to investigate for yourself. When the Buddha describes cessation, he is talking about the potential we all have to completely fulfill our fundamental, instinctive wish to be happy. The first set—the truth of suffering and the truth of origin—is easy enough to understand if we really contemplate it, but can the path that the Buddha describes really lead to the complete cessation of suffering? Is this possible, or is this merely Buddhist dogma, something we are being asked to accept unquestioningly simply because the Buddha said it?

Even if the first set feels true to us, will the path really lead to cessation? And if so, what is that cessation—complete extinction or existence on a different level? These are the questions we need to seriously consider.

Being Our Own Refuge

It is you who must make the effort. The Great of the past only show the way. Those who think and follow the path become free from the bondage of Mara.[4]

If we all have an instinctive wish for happiness, these words taken from the *Dhammapada* tell us where to begin the search to fulfill it. We are our own refuge. The key to fulfilling our need for happiness lies within, not outside, us. This means that we have all we need right here, inside, without looking to external things. And more good news—it's cheap! We don't have to pay for our happiness!

I cannot emphasize enough how powerful and accurate this verse is. Everybody, all the time, is trying to fulfill the instinctive wish to attain happiness and avoid unhappiness, and yet no one seems able to do so. Here, however, is the simple truth: the source of our own happiness is within ourselves.

We are still not really aware of the inner refuge that the Buddha says we should understand, because we have not reached the level where we can tap it. Until we do, we will continue looking for happiness outside, and there will be no way to satisfy that instinct. Bringing that internal refuge to life is what Dharma practice is all about.

It is really up to us. The Buddha says in the *Dhammapada* that we should work for our own liberation because the buddhas can only show us the way. They can give us the tools, but we must use them ourselves.

One very important point that the Buddha mentions in his first teaching is to avoid the two extremes, which are as follows:

> [t]he pursuit of sensual happiness in sensual pleasures, which is low, vulgar, the way of worldlings, ignoble, unbeneficial; and the pursuit of self-mortification, which is painful, ignoble, unbeneficial.

Because these two—excessive self-indulgence and excessive self-denial—are easy traps to fall into, it is very important to be clear about them. The Buddha's words in this case were directed at the five monks who were his first audience, but I think that these words are very valuable even outside the monastic context. They are relevant to our own daily lives. If we fall into one extreme, indulging ourselves in sense pleasures by merely living for sensory gratification, we devote our entire lives to something useless, robbing ourselves of any energy for what is worthwhile.

Self-mortification, the other extreme, seems an archaic concept in this material world, something more suited to the Indian forests of two thousand years ago. On the surface it seems that nobody we know punishes his or her body by not eating or drinking in order to find spiritual salvation. There are people, however, who push themselves too hard in their search for something spiritual, ending up sick and unhappy. And it is quite common to find people who mortify their bodies for worldly reasons, too. In both cases, self-denial is ego-driven.

Seeking sense pleasure is definitely the bigger danger for most of us. Our society and the media—especially advertising—promote the compulsion to indulge our sense pleasures. Advertisements are always saying, "You need this, you need that," whereas upon investigation it has nothing to do with need and everything to do with sensory gratification. There is a big difference, however, between devotion to sensory gratification and satisfying our daily needs. The Buddha says:

He who fills his lamp with water will not dispel the darkness, and he who tries to light a fire with rotten wood will fail. And how can anyone be free from self by leading a wretched life, if he does not succeed in quenching the fires of lust, if he still hankers after either worldly or heavenly pleasures. But he in whom self has become extinct is free from lust; he will desire neither worldly nor heavenly pleasures, and the satisfaction of his natural wants will not defile him. However let him be moderate, let him eat and drink according to the needs of the body.... To keep the body in good health is a duty, for otherwise we shall not be able to trim the lamp of wisdom and keep our mind strong and clear. Water surrounds the lotus flower but does not wet its petals.[5]

Growing out of mud and water, the petals of the lotus are still clean and dry. We live in the desire realm surrounded by the objects of our senses—our sight, hearing, smell, taste, and touch—but the sense objects do not have to drown us. At present they overwhelm us and rob us of time to practice Dharma. Also, they never really satisfy us—like drinking salt water, the more we drink, the more thirsty we become.

The Buddha's life is an example of the journey beyond both extremes. After his early palace life of utter sensory gratification, like many spiritual practitioners of the time, the Buddha deliberately deprived his body of what it needed in the belief that this could bring salvation. After six years the Buddha realized that this was not the way to fulfill his instinctive wish for happiness and freedom from suffering. He found that the only path was through what he called the *middle way*, which he summarized in his first teaching in the form of the noble eightfold path.

We need to be really clear on this ourselves before we even begin our journey. Is following the middle way, avoiding both extremes, the only way to fulfill our instinctive need for true happiness? And if that is so, what does following the middle way entail? If we are clear that it really leads to happiness, we will develop great motivation to sincerely follow this path. There is no doubt in my mind that this is so, and if Buddhadharma has even the potential to reduce the problems and difficulties we face these days, then it is our responsibility to do our utmost to practice it.

If that is true, it is also our duty to stay healthy. Without the body in good health we will not be able to "trim the lamp of wisdom" and keep our minds strong and clear, which is the first step in our exploration of our inner selves to find that well of happiness. This process depends on keeping the balance between the two extremes.

Responsibility to Ourselves and Others

When we observe how animals react if they are harmed even a little, we can see that they naturally try to protect themselves. Scientists say that this instinct to survive and avoid harm is a biological function. But our existence is more than that; it is a combination of our biology, emotions, sensations, and other mental components. It is very beneficial to observe what actions we perform in our daily lives. Ideally, we should be continually mindful, examining everything that we do and the intention we have while doing it.

Sometimes we may feel that we do things without any kind of con-scious intention. But if we are truly mindful, we can notice ourselves as we act; and if we trace the motivation back, we will definitely see that we have an instinctive wish to enhance our happiness or reduce our difficulties in some way. Through mindfulness we can glimpse this instinctive wish while it is arising.

We can even go further, recognizing that regardless of superficial differences, deep down all beings possess this same instinctive feeling: At this deepest of levels is complete equality among all sentient beings. Understanding this is fundamental if we want to truly help others.

In fact, if we naturally saw our motivation at such a deep level, we would not need to try to generate a good motivation; it would come effortlessly. We would simply know that all beings have as much right to happiness as we have, and we would naturally want to help them. This is the basis of ethics. His Holiness the Dalai Lama says:

> My own view, which does not rely solely on religious faith, nor even on an original idea, but rather on ordinary common sense, is that establishing binding ethical principles is possible when we take as our starting point the observation that we all desire happiness and wish to avoid suffering. We have no means of discriminating between right and wrong if we do not take into account others' feelings, others' suffering…[E]thical conduct is not something we engage in because it is somehow right in itself but because, like ourselves, all others desire hap-piness and to avoid suffering.[6]

I find his words very powerful. There can be no ethics—no sense of right or wrong—without taking others' feelings into account. Right from the beginning we should try to see that the feelings and rights of others are important and work toward serving not only our own welfare but also the welfare of all others.

Without any religious dogma whatsoever, by using simple common sense, it is important to judge what is right and what is wrong, what is happiness and what is unhappiness. We can only really do this if we can understand that the feelings, rights, and needs of others are every bit as important as our own.

2 THE TRUTH
   OF SUFFERING

Why the Buddha Began with the Teaching on Suffering

THE BUDDHA BEGAN his first teaching with the explanation of basic human suffering. He could have started instead with human aspirations— such as going to the beach, having a good holiday, or getting a big house—but he started with the opposite view, with suffering. Why? It is my personal feeling that this question should be treated very seriously.

Until the Buddha was an adult he knew nothing of suffering, being brought up as a prince amid unimaginable wealth, beauty, and splendor. And yet it was suffering that initiated his spiritual quest. The life story of the Buddha describes the way he was shocked out of complacency by seeing natural (but for him unknown) events such as sickness, old age, and death. Upon seeing a sick man, a dying man, and a corpse, he realized how hollow his life had been. With this shock came both the realization of the human condition and the wish to change it, and this point marks the beginning of the Buddha's great spiritual quest. He left his pampered environment in which all suffering was denied and where there was nothing but beauty.

The story of the Buddha happening upon the basic kinds of suffering is a perfect illustration of the first two noble truths. The shock of the outside world was necessary to awaken him from his sensually induced stupor, and as a result the Buddha left his wife, son, and possessions in search of the truth. Normally we do not even have the determination to give up our most basic comforts for something worthwhile, let alone abandon a beloved wife, child, and a life of total luxury. Prince Siddhartha had that determination because he was able to see how all suffering is brought about by what we call *conditioned existence* and how we are all equally subject to it. Conditioned existence refers to the pervasive way our lives, including our body and our thoughts, arise in dependence on contaminated past actions. Seeing this so clearly gave him inspiration, and he pursued the puzzle of conditioned existence unwaveringly until he found the way to end it.

I find that this story has a real resonance in Western society, where such things as birth, aging, sickness, and death are also hidden from view. Like the Buddha, we need to see that these things are in fact the reality of our lives and that fulfillment from chasing sense pleasures is not. Only when we truly understand the difficulties that face us now and in the future, and how deep-rooted they are, will we begin to actively seek a way out of suffering. We will only begin to really search for the end of our fundamental psychological dissatisfaction when we can clearly see how deeply it is rooted within us. Being told that fire burns might make us cautious, but standing with our hands in the fire will certainly give us ample incentive to take them out!

Only by investigating the nature of our underlying dissatisfaction can we come to see the whole story and, from that point, find a way out of our situation.

The Three Phases

> "Now this, bhikkhus, is the noble truth of suffering: birth is suffering, aging is suffering, illness is suffering, death is suffering; union with what is displeasing is suffering; separation

from what is pleasing is suffering; not to get what one wants is suffering; in brief, the five aggregates subject to clinging are suffering…

"'This noble truth of suffering is to be fully understood': thus, bhikkhus, in regard to things unheard before, there arose in me vision, knowledge, wisdom, true knowledge, and light.

"'This noble truth of suffering has been fully understood': thus, bhikkhus, in regard to things unheard before, there arose in me vision, knowledge, wisdom, true knowledge, and light."

As I mentioned in the previous chapter, the Buddha describes each of the four noble truths three times, as three *phases*. These three phases are particularly important in relation to the first noble truth. The first phase describes the nature of the truth of suffering, the second phase explains the importance of comprehending the specific significance of the truth of suffering for the practitioner, and the third phase explains the ultimate result or complete attainment of the truth of suffering—the complete recognition of suffering.

In relation to the first phase, the nature of the truth of suffering, the Buddha lists several different types of suffering that we all have to experience—birth, aging, and so forth—concluding with what he calls "the five aggregates subject to clinging." This group includes both physical and mental difficulties.

For our benefit, later Buddhist masters categorized them into different divisions, such as the three types of suffering and the eight types of suffering as presented in Lama Tsongkhapa's *Great Stages of the Path* (*Lamrim Chenmo*). We will look at these two sets later. These lists are intended to help us see what is here within us as clearly and accurately as we can.

We should understand that this is not the Buddha telling us to suffer, but rather an assertion that we need to understand suffering as it actually is. There are so many types of suffering to know about. The Buddha listed many, but, if we think about it, we can come up with even more—there seem to be infinite unpleasant things that confront us daily and an equal number of desirable things that are just out of reach. That is what the first phase explains.

The concept of suffering is a very subtle one, so much so that many books, instead of translating it, use the original word, *dukkha* in Pali or *duhkha* in Sanskrit. *Suffering* in English conveys only a gross level of meaning, and I can see why scholars are tempted to keep to the original or try other terms such as *dissatisfaction*. Dukkha means suffering at all levels. Of course everyday suffering *is* present—pain, difficulties, illness, and discomfort—but dukkha has more to do with psychological suffering, the sense of dissatisfaction that is very deeply rooted in our psyche. The Buddha's summary—that the five aggregates subject to clinging are suffering—really takes it to the deepest level. He means that everything about us, all of our mental and physical constituents, are suffering because we cling to them in some form.

The Buddha also talks about suffering as being separated from what we want and getting what we don't want. If we really examine our life, this is the norm rather than the exception, and it seems impossible for it to be otherwise. On the surface, life might be good, with plenty of excitement and distractions, with money in the bank and a good job, but scratch the surface and I guarantee you will find that hollow, empty feeling. It sometimes seems to me that a great part of Western life is a desperate cover-up that exists in order to repress this fundamental dissatisfaction.

The first phase of teaching on the first noble truth is simply as the Buddha said—to acknowledge suffering in all the ways it manifests; that is, to understand its identity.

When the Buddha said, "This noble truth of suffering is to be fully understood," he is taking us to the second phase of this truth, which is the importance of comprehending the specific significance of the truth of suffering. For people actively seeking liberation from suffering, knowing the types of suffering is not enough. Everything about the various sufferings needs to be understood—how they function, how we experience them individually and collectively, what their durations are, and so forth.

When the practitioner has fully understood all of the categories and levels of suffering, that understanding is the final understanding, which is the third phase. This understanding will remain on the mental continuum without any need to renew it in any way.

Types of Suffering

THE THREE TYPES OF SUFFERING

Coming to understand suffering or *dukkha* requires a lot of effort on our part. Suffering is far more than gross physical suffering. Westerners in particular tend to block any thoughts of suffering from the mind, in the belief that dwelling on the negative is a bad attitude. In fact, understanding the truth of suffering is actually appreciating the reality of our situation.

Suffering covers a vast spectrum of our experience, and the subtler it is, the harder it is to see it. In his teaching on the first noble truth, the Buddha taught three main levels of suffering that sentient beings experience. These are:

+ the suffering of suffering
+ the suffering of change
+ pervasive suffering

The suffering of suffering

Even animals understand the suffering of suffering. It is unpleasant and explicitly undesirable. Nobody runs after this form of suffering, and we need no sophisticated explanations to understand it. Nor do we need to devise skillful stratagems to avoid it—animals, insects, and humans are all constantly involved with doing so already, even though none of our attempts seems very skillful. We all wish to be free from this gross suffering.

I was in Sera Monastery when it was reconstructed in South India in 1970. Just a few meters from the monks' rooms was thick jungle full of wild animals and other dangers. The Indian government had started to clear the land to grow crops. Elephants were used to collect the cleared logs and put them onto trucks because they were very strong and well trained. Between Sera and the Tibetan camp were two streams with only two wooden bridges, and the elephants would invariably refuse to take a single step over them until they had checked the strength of the bridges with their trunks. They knew that falling from a bridge would bring suffering, and they were trying to avoid that suffering. This indicated to me that animals understand this level of suffering very well and actively try to avoid it.

The physical and mental pain we experience on this first level of suffering is easy to recognize and relatively easy to find a solution for. We do not have to adopt a spiritual practice to be free from it; it can be avoided through mundane methods with mundane understanding. When the Buddha said that suffering should be understood, of course he was including this kind of suffering, but he was mainly concerned with the deeper levels of suffering.

The suffering of change

The second level of suffering is the *suffering of change*. Because this level of suffering is much more subtle and not apparent without some analysis, it is more difficult to recognize. Without investigation, objects at this level actually appear to be causes of happiness, because they bring some temporary pleasure. However, if we have mindfulness, we can see them for what they are. Initially, things and events (such as relationships, possessions, and so forth) appear desirable—they look as if they will bring happiness. That's why we become attracted to them. However, when time passes and circumstances change, the same desirable, handsome, beautiful object turns into something ugly or undesirable—something we want to avoid. We've all had that kind of experience, and if we have enough mindfulness this will be quite obvious. This is the suffering of change—due to the changing situation, our view of the object or event also changes.

Buddhism posits that everything is impermanent and that change brings suffering because we want things to remain as they are. We are therefore facing problems all the time, whether we see them as problems at that moment or not.

To gain insight into how this happens, we need an understanding of the gross level of impermanence—how things come into being, remain, and then cease by the power of things other than themselves. Things arise by the power of others, and while they remain they are still under the power of others. Their cessation also depends on the power of others. Nothing happens independently. Understanding this gross level of impermanence and the fact that we actually have so little freedom will help us understand the more subtle levels of impermanence.

We all know that things change, but we need to understand this at more than an intellectual level—we must understand it instinctively, emotionally. Change has the potential to bring suffering, but it is important to realize that change is not suffering by nature. There is a big difference. The change from autumn to winter is nothing more than that—the change from autumn to winter. There are no emotions involved in the change of weather at all. It is only when our emotions come into the picture that the potential for suffering arises. We have aversion to the cold and gray of winter and cling to the last of the beautiful days, and so the change makes us suffer. It is not the change that is suffering but our attachment to pleasant things and our wish that they remain that turns to suffering when we lose them or are threatened with their loss.

There is nothing wrong with enjoyment, but when we are attracted to something we have to bear in mind that it will change. Very often we are either not aware of this or we deny this changing nature, and then when the change comes, as it must, it comes as a huge shock to us. Our parents might be very old and in nursing homes, but when they die it is as if they have cheated us in some way.

Buddhist explanations are always rational, whereas our minds are not always so. Although we might seem slaves to our irrational, spontaneous emotions, it really does help to look at what is happening to us in as rational and logical a way as possible. Understanding our minds, we can slowly learn to lessen the effect that unwanted emotions have on them, and through constant effort, we can avoid falling prey to strong emotions that lead to great suffering.

Pervasive suffering

The third level of suffering is *pervasive suffering*. It is the most important level from a Buddhist point of view, and to really understand it we need a very thorough explanation. This is the level of suffering that the Buddha is primarily referring to when he says that suffering should be understood. The Buddha concludes his description of the first noble truth with "The five aggregates subject to clinging are suffering." Since our existence is nothing more than these five aggregates—our body and our mental states—this indicates how truly integrated suffering is with our very being. *Pervasive* means that this suffering pervades our entire existence.

This level of suffering, and the causes and conditions that bring it about, can be understood through the teachings on the subtle levels of impermanence. Pervasive suffering is present wherever we are born in cyclic existence; we cannot avoid it. And yet, because its causes and conditions are very deeply rooted, it is very difficult for us, as ordinary people, to even recognize it and acknowledge at all. However, only when we acknowledge it we can begin to abandon it. The effects of pervasive suffering spread throughout our lives and often manifest in the form of grosser sufferings, which makes it difficult for us to really come to grips with it. It is so enmeshed that even understanding it, let alone overcoming it, takes a lot of effort.

Of pervasive suffering His Holiness the Dalai Lama says:

> This addresses the main question: why is this the nature of things? The answer is, because everything that happens in samsara is due to ignorance.... Here the third level of suffering therefore refers to the bare fact of our unenlightened existence.[7]

This third level of suffering is actually our unenlightened existence itself, which is under the influence of fundamental confusion and negative karma. Therefore, nothing within our existence is excluded from this third level of suffering. The best instrument to further understand pervasive suffering is an understanding of impermanence.

The Theravada writer Walpola Rahula says:

> It is *dukkha* not because there is suffering in the ordinary sense of the word, but because whatever is impermanent is *dukkha*.[8]

Literally, Rahula asserts that you are suffering at this moment, while reading this, because you are impermanent.

Tibetan Buddhism phrases it slightly differently, asserting that because something is contaminated, it is therefore suffering. This assertion does not have quite the same connotation as the statement, "Whatever is impermanent is suffering," because it allows for impermanent things that are not contaminated.

If we examine impermanence merely on a gross level—the way we age, the way our possessions fall apart—then it certainly seems that all impermanent things are suffering. However, when we understand the more subtle levels of impermanence, we will see that this is not actually so. The classic example used in debate in the Tibetan system is the enlightened mind. The enlightened mind is a kind of mind, and hence impermanent. If we say that a person, through practice, becomes an enlightened being, then using that argument we must say that that mind, which is enlightened, would have to be dukkha, because it is impermanent. This is obviously illogical. This point illustrates one of the main differences between Theravada and Mahayana. According to the Theravada tradition, when an individual practitioner manages to overcome all suffering and achieves full liberation or nirvana, that person ceases; he or she literally becomes completely nonexistent.

The Mahayana tradition does not accept this. Instead, it asserts that it is the defilements within the mind that cease rather than the mind itself. Remember the example in the previous chapter of the cup that is empty of tea, which exemplifies the cessation of suffering as a state of existence. That state of cessation is permanent. The mind that is free of suffering, however, does not ceases to exist.

Pervasive suffering refers to that unsatisfactory state that pervades our entire unenlightened existence. We will not be free of it until we are free from samsara, until we are buddhas.

THE EIGHT TYPES OF SUFFERING

The eight types of suffering are:

1. the suffering of birth
2. the suffering of old age
3. the suffering of illness
4. the suffering of death
5. the suffering of encountering what is unpleasant
6. the suffering of separation from what is pleasant
7. the suffering of not getting what you want
8. the suffering of the five appropriated aggregates.[9]

In Lama Tsongkhapa's *Great Stages of the Path*, the eight types of suffering are explained thoroughly. For example, the first type of suffering—the suffering of birth—is divided into four points. The first point is obvious—birth is suffering because it is associated with pain. Although we probably cannot remember our own birth, I personally remember the births of my sister and two brothers, who were born before I entered the monastery. I well recall how they came into this world. They were screaming very loudly, which really shows the physical discomfort they were experiencing.

Birth is suffering not only because it is associated with pain, but also because it is a condition for future suffering. The day we are born is the beginning of all of the difficulties we will experience in this lifetime. Therefore, to a certain extent, the propensities or seeds of future suffering that we carry within our mindstreams are triggered as a result of birth in this type of body. In this way, birth is the beginning of our suffering.

The third point is that birth is suffering because it is the origin of suffering. The day we are born is the day we start aging and the day we start moving toward the mental and physical discomfort and illness that we will surely experience in this life. It is also the day we begin our inexorable journey toward death. Therefore, to a certain extent, the three sufferings that follow the suffering of birth—old age, illness, and death—are triggered by birth. Birth is also suffering because it is an experience of unwanted separation from the safety of the mother's womb, which is in turn the precursor to the unwanted separation from this lifetime that we will eventually experience when we die.

Lama Tsongkhapa explains the other types of suffering in similar detail. These points can be very useful tools in meditation if we really want to take this subject seriously. It is helpful to look at our lives in light of this depiction and allow it to penetrate our experience. The complete subject matter is far too extensive to go into here, but I strongly recommend that you read and study books on Lama Tsongkhapa's *Great Stages of the Path,* particularly the section that explains the stages of the path for a person of medium capacity.[10]

THE FIVE AGGREGATES

We are nothing other than our bodies and minds. Traditionally these two are divided into five *heaps* or aggregates—form, feeling, discrimination, compositional factors, and consciousness. *Form* here means our body, and the other aggregates are all facets of the mind. In this instance I am using Tibetan Buddhist terminology, but in the Theravada texts you might find different words—such as sensation and perception. The meaning is the same.

The five aggregates are the sum total of what we are, so understanding them is integral to seeing the totality of the suffering we experience. I suffer—that is undeniable, but who is the "I" that experiences that suffering? Working through each of the five aggregates, we can try to pinpoint the "I," or the lack of it, and arrive finally at the conclusion that no "me," "I," or "I who am suffering" can be found.

Recognizing this reality directly is quite advanced, but knowing the concept of the five aggregates is the starting point.

The form aggregate includes all of the physical aspects of our bodies. The feeling aggregate is the raw, unprocessed positive, negative, or neutral sensation that we experience when we first perceive an object, and the discrimination aggregate refers to the interpretation and labeling of that raw sensation into concepts such as "friend," "father," "beautiful," and so on. Discrimination can also be called *perception*.

The fourth aggregate, *compositional factors* or *mental formations*, includes many different types of mental processes, such as doubt, desire, determination, conceit, and so forth. Particularly important among these is the process of volition, or karma. The fifth aggregate, consciousness, includes the five sensory consciousnesses—seeing, hearing, smelling, tasting, and touching—and mental consciousness. *Consciousness* here means the simple fact of awareness, the capacity for experience. There is absolutely nothing outside of these five aggregates that we can call "me." Our present unenlightened existence is composed only of these five aggregates.

Overall, in our day-to-day lives, how aware are we of these five aggregates, and how aware are we that our existence is entirely composed of them? These five physical and mental aggregates are the complete "me," and they are definitely subject to change. We suffer as a consequence of our resistance to that change. Although we may not feel we deserve to suffer, we are subject to suffering because this is our nature. In fact, by nature we are totally under the influence of the causes and conditions that ripen due to our karmic dispositions. In Buddhism this is called *other-powered*. Our current five aggregates are contaminated because they are products of ignorance and delusion. Very simply, because our aggregates are contaminated, we suffer.

The Four Characteristics of the Truth of Suffering

In the Mahayana tradition, each noble truth possesses four character-istics, making sixteen in all. Commentaries such as the *Ornament of Clear Realization (Abhisamayalamkara)* by Maitreya explain these char-acteristics as a meditation guide to be practiced during the path to enlightenment. For our purposes, it is especially important to under-stand the characteristics of the noble truth of suffering:

+ impermanence
+ suffering
+ emptiness
+ selflessness

IMPERMANENCE

Very often Buddhism talks about this first characteristic, imperma-nence, in connection with death. Of course if we have some idea of impermanence, we can handle death more easily, but the main reason to seek an understanding of impermanence is to understand that attachment to the five aggregates is suffering.

To understand pervasive suffering we have to understand how these different levels of impermanence work. Generally, we do under-stand that things come and go. They arise due to causes and condi-tions, remain until their lifespan is finished, and then they are extinguished. On this level, it is not difficult to understand that things are impermanent. Beyond that, however, there is a more subtle level of impermanence of which we must become aware. This level is called *changing moment by moment,* referring to the fact that things do not stay the same for even one moment. Again, this is not so dif-ficult to understand.

The aspect of impermanence that poses the greatest challenge to our understanding is the fact that when phenomena come into being due to causes and conditions, those same causes and conditions that produce them, *at the same moment*, contain the seeds of their own destruction. In a BBC program on the human body a few years ago, a scientist said that genes destroy themselves through the process of being created; simultaneous with their formation, they begin to break apart. This is similar to the Buddhist idea that within the very act of creation is the seed of destruction.

We can take as an example the impermanence of a table. It is easy enough to see that a table comes into being through the collection of causes and conditions, and that a time will come when it will no longer exist; it will be destroyed by the process of natural disintegration or by other forces, such as somebody burning it. From the Buddhist point of view, however, from the moment of the table's creation, it is not static but moves inexorably toward disintegration. This indicates that the causes and conditions that produce that phenomenon contain the seed for its destruction. Herein lies the potential for suffering. The table, right at the beginning, comes into being through the power of other things—it cannot produce itself. In the same way, everything is other-powered. Everything relies on other powers, other factors to come into being, and that dependence makes things subject to disintegration.

At present I am the resident teacher at Jamyang Buddhist Centre in London, and my contract with the center imposes certain limits on me. My residence at Jamyang is totally dependent on the power of others, and that fact imposes some kind of restriction. Whether I like it is a different issue, involving other emotions, but in itself this situation imposes limits and that is a kind of suffering. I am not saying that the table is unhappy being a table, or that I am unhappy being a resident teacher. But the simple fact that I am under the control of other forces induces a subtle level of suffering.

We do not have to go as far as looking at the emptiness of the table or of Geshe Tashi. If we look at mere existence alone we will see that it is, as His Holiness puts it, *unenlightened existence*. Our present unenlightened existence is totally under the power of ignorance and delusions and totally given to uncontrolled change. For this reason, we can understand that our present unenlightened state is dukkha.

SUFFERING

From the Buddhist point of view, our present existence came into being due to ignorance and afflictive emotions (for more on afflictive emotions, see page 64). This is the second of the four aspects of the noble truth of suffering: suffering.

We need to understand this very clearly. In our present unenlightened state, just having the five aggregates is suffering because they are produced by the fundamental confusion of ignorance and afflictive emotions, and therefore there is no basis for pure happiness in them. Our basic composition is imperfect, so how can we expect perfect happiness?

However, we are looking to be free from samsara, so we also need to understand that within our mindstreams exists the potential for us to produce the causes and conditions required for liberation. Since in our everyday lives we find it very hard to differentiate between what is real happiness and what is real suffering, understanding this potential can really help us.

In ancient India many practitioners of non-Buddhist traditions believed that full spiritual attainment was synonymous with the development of perfect concentration, a state of mind in which all sensations, and hence the sensory levels of suffering, cease. Through concentration we can reduce and finally eliminate the awareness of all sensory objects, and taking this to the ultimate will lead to rebirth in a realm with no sensory objects whatsoever.

At present, we live in what is called the *desire realm*, because the beings who reside there are dominated by the senses: seeing, hearing, smelling, tasting, and touching. At every moment, waking or sleeping, our minds grasp at sensation in one form or another. Beings of the *formless realm* have transcended this state, and are beyond even those who live in the intermediate *form realm*, where there are very few sensory objects. The formless realm is created by perfect concentration, a realm totally free of sensation. As I noted above, certain non-Buddhist traditions consider the attainment of this realm the ultimate spiritual attainment. However, while the Buddhist tradition accepts the possibility of rebirth in the formless realm as a result of flawless concentration, it questions whether that attainment marks the end of suffering; Buddhists consider the formless realm as still within cyclic existence. Although there may be no gross suffering in that state, beings born there still possess four of the five contaminated aggregates (they have no form aggregate) and hence are still subject to suffering.

And so we see that suffering is almost impossible to avoid, and that where there is mind or form arising from delusions and karma, it is totally impossible.

EMPTINESS

Emptiness, the third characteristic of the first noble truth, refers to the emptiness of a self that is a permanent, unitary, and indivisible reality. Many people have a notion of a soul or "self" as something individual, and believe there is some unchanging thing within our ever-changing aggregates—something separate from both body and mind—that holds the essence of "me." This characteristic of emptiness—that there is no "I" separate from the aggregates—is a very gross level of selflessness.

We are always identifying with the "I," and we always associate the "I" with one of the five aggregates. It is this attachment to the aggregates that should be understood to be suffering and abandoned. In order to understand that, we have to understand that this thing we call "I," according to Buddhist philosophy, is only the combination of ever-changing physical and mental phenomena and events.

Selflessness

The fourth characteristic, selflessness, refers to the lack of existence of any self-supporting, independent, substantially existing person. This is not how we see things. In contrast, we instinctively feel that we are more than just the combination of mental and physical aggregates; we are certain that there is something there that is a self-supporting identity, a self that is a self-sufficient, substantial reality.

The previous characteristic, emptiness, refutes the wrong notion of a self that is completely independent of the five aggregates. The characteristic of selflessness refutes the wrong notion of a self that can be found within the five aggregates and yet is still self-sufficient or substantial. The difference between these two wrong views can be exemplified by the analogy of the difference between a king and the chief executive of a big company. In our usual conception of "me and my five aggregates," we often feel like a controller with the aggregates under our control, much as a king controls his subjects. The king remains in his castle, utterly separate from his subjects but totally in control. The third characteristic, emptiness, refutes this wrong notion of a self that is totally independent of the aggregates by saying that it is empty of such an independent existence.

In other contexts we might instinctively feel that we are not separate from our aggregates but still in control, in the same way a business executive, like the other workers, is also human and works in the office but is somehow special because he is in control. Similarly, the fourth characteristic, selflessness, refutes the wrong notion that while the self is not totally independent of the aggregates, it is nevertheless self-sufficient within them.

The third characteristic is gross, while the fourth is far more subtle. It is not a difficult logical exercise to see that this "I" that we cherish so dearly cannot exist apart from the aggregates, that it has to be in some way dependent on the collection of body and mind. There can be no king over there controlling the subjects over here. However, although we might be capable of understanding this point, it is much more difficult to see that, even within the five aggregates, there is no self-existent "I" at all.

If the difference between *empty of self* and *selfless* seems like splitting hairs, you should know that as you go deeper into Buddhist psychology and the theories of emptiness, this distinction will become more important. Whereas all Buddhist philosophical schools agree that there is no "I" apart from the five aggregates, two lower schools, the Vaibhashika and Sautrantika, assert that there is nonetheless some substantially existing entity that we can posit as an "I."

Within the highest school, the Madhyamaka, we examine each of the aggregates one by one and see that our physical form cannot be the "I," nor our feelings, and so forth. Seeing that no single aggregate can be the "I" and yet understanding that we instinctively see the "I" as a singularity, Madhyamikas posit that it exists only as a label for our ever-changing body and mind. Nagarjuna uses the term *merely labeled* to describe how this works.

There is no question that self exists; all Buddhist scholars assert that this is so, simply because we have experiences. But the concept of selflessness refutes the common misunderstanding that within the five aggregates there is a substantially existing "I". This kind of self does not exist.

So often, out of confusion, we identify one of these five aggregates as "me" and then suffer because of it. Understanding the characteristics of emptiness and selflessness helps us to overcome that confusion. It is important to remember, too, that it is our attachment to the five aggregates that causes suffering, not the aggregates themselves. That is why we really need wisdom. We do not have to go as far as a direct realization of emptiness to gain some understanding of the true nature of self; through applying our intellectual analysis to the mindful awareness of our own experiences, we can begin right now to reduce our suffering.

Contemplating these four characteristics one by one, we come to understand our lives more clearly, and we learn to differentiate between our normal perceptions and how things really are.

Understanding the Truth of Suffering in Our Everyday Lives

THERE IS SUFFERING

Arguments about aggregates and dukkha might seem very esoteric and abstract, but understanding the relationship between the self and the aggregates is vital if we are really going to turn our lives around and start to rise above our suffering. If the self were a mere label on the five aggregates and the aggregates were nothing but suffering, our situation would be quite bleak. To eliminate suffering, we would have to eliminate the aggregates and hence cease to exist!

The Theravada and Mahayana traditions have a basic difference of opinion on this point, which seems to stem from the way the *Four Noble Truths Sutra* is interpreted, specifically the phrase "the five aggregates subject to clinging are suffering." For Theravada writers such as Walpola Rahula, this means that dukkha and the five aggregates are not different; the aggregates themselves are dukkha. Mahayana scholars, on the other hand, read this to mean that it is not the five aggregates themselves that are suffering, but *attachment* to the five aggregates.

In the *Introduction to the Middle Way (Madhyamakavatara)* Chandrakirti says of the Theravada idea of self:

> Some assert all five aggregates as the basis of the view of self,
> And some assert the mind alone.[11]

He argues that if the aggregates were suffering, and if the self were either within or the same as the five aggregates, then liberation from suffering would be impossible. Because our ultimate goal is to extinguish all suffering, then that would mean total annihilation through extinguishing the aggregates. Is this buddhahood?

According to the Theravada tradition, when the historical Buddha, Buddha Shakyamuni, attained enlightenment under the Bodhi tree, his physical body, and the rest of his aggregates, were still dukkha. But within the Mahayana tradition, and especially within the tantric Vajrayana, which is part of the Mahayana, the five aggregates have many different levels, some very subtle. In fact, in the Vajrayana, one level of the five aggregates represents the five so-called *dhyani buddhas,* the five primordial energies. Therefore, according to the Mahayana, it is possible to have aggregates that are totally uncontaminated. We need to explore all these different ideas, and discern for ourselves whether Buddha Shakyamuni was a normal human being who attained enlightenment or an already-enlightened being who came to our world system to show us the path to enlightenment.

Ajahn Sumedho, a wonderful Theravada teacher, very skillfully suggests that we should not think that we *are* suffering, but rather that there *is* suffering. This is very good advice for people at our level, because by doing this we avoid having to think about whether the "I" is the same as the aggregates. To meditate "I am suffering," we need an "I." Through meditating in this more impersonal way, we can become aware of the universality of suffering within every moment of experience. Aging and death are very gross manifestations of suffering. But through meditation on the various manifestations of suffering within our aggregates, we can get at suffering's more fundamental levels.

In *The Three Principles of the Path*, Lama Tsongkhapa wrote a beautiful verse that describes our present situation.

> Swept by the current of the four powerful rivers,
> Tied by strong bonds of karma, so hard to undo,
> Caught in the iron net of self-grasping,
> Completely enveloped by the darkness of ignorance.[12]

This is the true situation of unenlightened beings. In the first line, we see our present situation, wherein we are borne along by these four different kinds of sufferings: birth, aging, sickness, and death. Our life starts with birth, which is full of pain and suffering, and ends with death, which is also suffering. Between these two, whether our life is short or long, sickness and aging keep punishing us. We are drowning in the currents of these four rivers, tossed around by strong waves.

The second line tells us that besides this, we are bound tightly by our past actions, the effects of which are inescapable. The third line describes the locus of our suffering still further, alluding to the imprisonment wrought by the ignorance that misunderstands the ego. Finally comes our most fundamental confusion, the ignorance of not knowing the reality of things and events. Unenlightened beings have many layers of suffering.

LETTING GO OF CLINGING TO PROBLEMS

It is quite common to deny the extent of suffering in our lives and pretend that everything is pretty much all right. As a result, when we first start to study Buddhism and investigate the state of our minds, it can seem that life is much worse than we previously believed. That's true, actually, but it is a necessary step. For only by starting to see things as they really are can we address the problem effectively. Suffering is present, internally and externally, whether we are Buddhist or not. The big difference now, however, is that in having some understanding of this first noble truth, we have the potential to perceive our situation accurately and find a solution.

Whether we actually do this is another matter, of course, and the test of our practice is how we handle problems. We all know what usually happens when we face difficulties—we experience impatience and anger, we blame others, and we deploy an artillery of defensive strategies. Although other people may contribute to our problems, the main cause is internal. Failing to see that, we place the blame on others. There may be some grim satisfaction from blaming the rest of the world for our problems, but this satisfaction is very shallow and very harmful, because it blocks us from full knowledge of the truth of suffering and the other noble truths.

The Buddha did not end his explanation after the first set of cause and effect (the truths of suffering and its origin). If he had, I think Buddhist practitioners would be quite gloomy compared to other spiritual practitioners, thinking the world is nothing but suffering. Instead the Buddha continued. After teaching the first set of cause and effect, he then taught the second set—the truths of cessation and the path to cessation. The third and fourth noble truths inspire us to do something more, rather than just making us feel depressed. And because the Buddha taught the second set of cause and effect, we need not feel hopeless, because a method to cure the problem exists.

Clinging to a problem does not make it disappear, but rather just makes it worse, aggravating the problem and leading to frustration and anger in relation to the problem and even in relation to ourselves. Having a tooth pulled might be painful, but it is nothing compared to the agony of sitting in the waiting room dreading it. When others harm us, fixating on the injustice of the situation or on others' cruelty just creates more problems in our minds. Often the animosity and annoyance we feel is far worse than the situation that caused it.

In this area I find the Theravada advice very good: let it go. Letting go might be hard, but it is really much easier than clinging, at least in the long run. Realizing that this problem is only temporary, like all things, and it too will pass, gives us more space to find ways to resolve it. This is the nice side of impermanence: The things we love might not last forever, but neither do the things that cause us problems.

Letting go is good in theory, but it is not easy to do because we are not used to it. One technique is to look at the problem from many angles—examine how it arose, how our own mental state contributed to it, what the other person's position is, and so forth. Rather than obsessing about the problem and how to get rid of it as quickly as possible, if we instead analyze our role in bringing this situation about, there is a greater chance that we will be able to let it go. Looking at the external conditions alone, seeing the problem as externally created, blocks us from seeing its real cause. Using our wisdom instead and focusing on our own mind and its role in the situation, we can see how the main cause is internal, and that makes it much easier to let go.

Meditating on the First Noble Truth

The Buddha said that the truth of suffering should be fully understood, and I feel that this means skillfully integrating our understanding of suffering into our daily lives. In *Lines of Experience*, the shortest of his three texts on the gradual path to enlightenment, Lama Tsongkhapa said that if we do not make an effort to think about true suffering but merely withdraw from seeking samsaric pleasures, we can never develop an interest in working for liberation. Simply denying ourselves pleasure is suppressing desire and will never work. The root cause is still there. However, by truly seeing the disadvantages of suffering, we naturally withdraw from the causes of suffering. And if we put effort into avoiding true suffering, the outcome is liberation.

Deeply understanding the truth of suffering means meditating on it, and there are many ways of doing this. Generally, the type of meditation we use to gain realization on this point is *analytical meditation*. When we think about something, which is virtually all the time, there is the mind and there is what we think about, the mind's object. If we structure this activity by intentionally focusing on a particular object, it becomes analytical meditation. In another type of meditation we try to make our mind *become* the object, such as when we meditate on compassion and try to become compassion. With analytical meditation, however, the subject—the mind—observes the object as a separate entity.

One method of meditating on the first noble truth is to meditate on the complete range of the disadvantages of cyclic existence, such as can be found in the teachings on the gradual path to enlightenment (Tib. *lamrim*). Some people find it easier to meditate on others' problems than on their own, so the meditations might focus on the sufferings of animals, hungry ghosts, and hell beings. For other people, meditating on their own problems makes more sense. Although the lamrim expounds on a vast range of sufferings, it is not necessary to meditate on every single one. Use whichever suffering is most com-pelling to you and makes your meditation most effective, and try to understand the destructive effects of that suffering—physically and mentally, short-term and long-term. Doing this will motivate you to do whatever is necessary to free yourself from that kind of state.

We can also meditate on how, for every desirable object we obtain, a related undesirable object comes into existence at the same time, and how it is therefore impossible to escape suffering as long as we continue to grasp onto pleasure. This is a meditation on the suffering of change, the second of the three basic types of suffering. Again, as this is analytical meditation, it is not that your mind *becomes* that suf-fering of change, but rather that you try to realize it as true or valid in light of your own experience.

Our lives are subject to three polarities:

+ satisfaction and dissatisfaction
+ attraction and aversion
+ freedom and lack of freedom

It is important to remember that where there is attraction, there is also aversion; that dissatisfaction goes along with satisfaction; and that if we have freedom we also lack freedom. Here I am referring to the relative freedom within samsara—freedom from domination, from financial worries, from sickness, and so forth—not the freedom or lib-eration that is nirvana. The point is that everything within samsara also carries with it the basis for its opposite. The same object that brings some kind of satisfaction will also eventually bring dissatisfac-tion. And the same object that binds us in samsara also has the power to liberate us. When we seek satisfaction, that very mind contains within it the seeds of future dissatisfaction, because a degree of igno-rance there clings to an unrealistic and unrealizable expectation. When we are attracted to something or someone, our mind exaggerates the qualities of that object, and so sets the scenario for future frustration and aversion to arise. In our daily activities we are constantly trying to attain one of these goals and avoid its opposite, but this is a fundamentally impossible quest. By analyzing this situation, we will realize the suffering of change.

One particularly useful meditation we can do is to analyze the five aggregates and examine their relationship to suffering. Looking first at the form aggregate, we can see how it acts as the foundation of so many of our problems. All of our physical problems, such as disease, headaches, and aging, are aspects of the body's natural process; they all come into being because we have a body.

Our exploration of the form aggregate can be linked with *uncertainty*, the first of the six general sufferings of samsara.[13] Even though we might think our bodies are strong and healthy now, it is impossible to predict what they will be like in a few years. This uncertainty creates anxiety, even subconsciously. By thinking about these issues again and again, slowly taking such awareness deeper until we can finally channel it into a single point, we will become firmly convinced that this form aggregate really is the foundation of all our problems.

We need to think about these things before we move onto the other aggregates and see how in the same way our mind is the cause of so many of our problems. Understanding that our existence started with the suffering of birth and will end with the suffering of death, and that in between we will experience many different kinds of suffering, we gain some measure of strength to not become discouraged when problems arise. They are part of the natural process of our lives, and as such they come and go.

We need to use every tool at our disposal to try to understand the noble truth of suffering at the deepest possible level. This is the Buddha's very clear message—that this noble truth describes our lives and needs to be understood. We can do that by seeing how our suffering comes from fundamental misunderstandings, such as believing that there is permanence where none exists and from misconceiving the nature of our identity. The more profound our understanding of suffering is the closer we will come to freeing ourselves from its yoke.

3 THE TRUTH OF ORIGIN

Delusions

THE THREE PHASES

"Now this, bhikkhus, is the noble truth of the origin of suffering: it is this craving that leads to renewed existence, accompanied by delight and lust, seeking delight here and there; that is, craving for sensual pleasures, craving for existence, craving for extermination...

"'This noble truth of the origin of suffering is to be abandoned': thus, bhikkhus, in regard to things unheard before, there arose in me vision, knowledge, wisdom, true knowledge, and light.

"'This noble truth of the origin of suffering has been abandoned': thus, bhikkhus, in regard to things unheard before, there arose in me vision, knowledge, wisdom, true knowledge, and light."

AS WITH THE OTHER noble truths, the noble truth of the origin of suffering is explained by the Buddha in three phases: the nature of the origin of suffering, what needs to be done in connection with the origin of suffering—it needs to be abandoned—and the compete attainment or final result, its abandonment.

The first phase lists different types of attachment (called *cravings* in the *Four Noble Truths Sutra*) that lead to renewed existence. These deep-rooted attachments are the main origins of suffering and, as practitioners seeking liberation from suffering, it is essential for us to know them. This enumeration was expanded upon by later Indian, Tibetan, and other Buddhist masters in order to give us as clear an understanding as possible of the source of our suffering. The Tibetan system in particular structures it very logically, showing how fundamental ignorance leads to afflictive emotions and karmic actions, which together are the cause of suffering. We cannot hope to dismantle any deep-rooted problems until we clearly understand this causal structure, and so this first phase of understanding is a prerequisite to the second phase of abandoning.

Abandoning the causes of suffering is the second phase of this noble truth. Of course it is not enough to simply understand why we suffer— we need to do something about it. Thus we need the motivation, which comes from realizing the importance of abandoning not just the superficial problems and their gross causes and conditions, but the more entrenched delusions and their very subtle origins as well. Again, the sutra merely states that the origin of suffering should be abandoned, while later masters go into great detail about the sequence of abandoning suffering.

In saying that the origin of suffering has been abandoned, the third phase explains the ultimate result—complete attainment. Using the right antidotes to utterly eliminate the source of suffering from the mental continuum, complete attainment is the final result; those sources will not resurface in the future. Thus the third phase says that the origin of suffering has been abandoned.

Because the origin of suffering is an object to be abandoned, it is helpful to not only understand what that origin is, but also how it creates very subtle levels of disturbance in our minds, which in turn are the origins of less subtle levels of suffering.

What we are experiencing now is suffering, which is a result. In whatever form that suffering manifests, its origin lies at the deepest level within the fundamental confusion about how things actually exist. This is called *ignorance*, but this is much more profound than the way the term is generally used in English. Two types of ignorance trigger all other problems: the ignorance of selflessness of persons and of phenomena. We will explore these later.

This fundamental ignorance leads to the creation of our afflictive emotions—attachment and aversion—which in turn lead us to create karmic actions and suffering. You often hear that suffering is caused by karma and delusions. *Delusions* is a blanket term for the combination of ignorance and the afflictive emotions of attachment and aversion. In Sanskrit it is *klesha*, which is sometimes also just used for afflictive emotions.

Having said that, in our everyday lives all these forces act simultaneously and continuously, making it appear that there is no logical sequence. There must be a sequence, however, because of the causal nature of suffering. There cannot be a result without a cause, and it is through the interaction of ignorance, afflictive emotions, and karmic actions that we experience the result of suffering. However, we need a high degree of awareness to appreciate this sequence.

IGNORANCE

The fundamental cause of suffering is ignorance. *Ignorance* is a term that comes up frequently in Buddhism, often without explanation since it is such a basic concept. It is vital to know what this *ignorance* actually refers to. Ignorance can be defined on many levels. It can refer to simply not understanding something fully and acting unskillfully as a result. This is the most superficial kind of ignorance, and there are layers and layers beneath this, down to the subtlest subconscious level of mind. In this context ignorance means our basis misapprehension of the nature of reality.

Ignorance is the ignition key, the starting point of the whole of cyclic existence. Because this deluded mind misunderstands reality, gross or subtle deluded emotions arise. Then, as a result of these afflictive emotions, we mentally, verbally, or physically react. The result of this is suffering.

Fundamental confusion

Practitioners of the Theravada and Mahayana traditions share a common understanding of the definition of the origin of suffering. The sutra states:

> "Now this, bhikkhus, is the noble truth of the origin of suffering: it is this craving that leads to renewed existence, accompanied by delight and lust, seeking delight here and there; that is, craving for sensual pleasures, craving for existence, craving for extermination."

In Pali the word for craving is *tanha*, which literally means "thirst." This concept seems to me to be the crucial term in the Theravada system, the term that points to the root of all our suffering. There is a strong emphasis on craving or thirst because it is a major cause of suffering, although Theravada scholars acknowledge that it is not the only cause. Walpola Rahula calls it the "most palpable and immediate cause."[14] The emphasis within Mahayana is slightly different. Thirst is seen as an origin, but the root source of our suffering is said to be our fundamental ignorance or confusion.

It is important not to feel that one explanation is "right" and the other "wrong," or that one is more profound and that therefore the other should be ignored. Likewise, we should not discard one explanation because it is Mahayana and does not suit us personally, or the other because it is Theravada and we call ourselves Tibetan Buddhists. Like so much in Buddhism, different explanations are designed to cater to people of diverse interests and dispositions. Some of us use Buddhism as a tool to make sense of our busy lives and have neither the time nor the inclination to delve into the more esoteric philosophies. We are searching for ways to keep our lives under control and gain some degree of peace. Others might have an opportunity for deeper study or the wish to put the teachings into practice in more depth and want to go a bit further than that. It is very helpful to read up on the different traditions and search for common ground, and then from that basis choose whichever is suitable for your own mentality and your own lifestyle. It is really what speaks to you at this moment that will help you.

Tracing back through the different layers of problems, we can see that our immediate suffering has a cause, but that this cause itself also has a cause. Very often you hear in Buddhist teachings that suffering is caused by karma and delusions. Karma is the seed that ripens into suffering. But karmic actions are triggered by our delusions, which themselves can be broken down into our afflictive emotions and the fundamental confusion that is the root cause.

Ignorance of the law of causality

When discussing the cause of suffering, terms such as *delusion* or *afflictive emotion* or *defilement* are often used quite loosely. However, the underlying cause of suffering is fundamental ignorance, of which His Holiness the Dalai Lama says:

[a]t the root of the situation lies a fundamental confusion, or in Buddhist terminology, a fundamental ignorance. This confusion applies not only to the way things are but also to the way causes and effects relate to each other. Therefore in Buddhism we talk about two types of ignorance or *avidya*: ignorance of the laws of causality, specifically the laws of karma, and ignorance of the ultimate nature of reality.[15]

The second ignorance that His Holiness mentions, ignorance of the ultimate nature of reality, refers to our lack of understanding of emptiness, which is a vast subject. For now I will just touch on the first type of ignorance, the ignorance of the law of causality, looking at what kind of ignorance it is and how we misunderstand it. In general, this ignorance can be divided into two categories: acquired ignorance and innate ignorance.

As the name implies, acquired ignorance is not intrinsic but rather comes about due to the influence of adopted beliefs and the culture we are raised in. We are influenced all the time, sometimes very persuasively, even if we are not conscious of it happening. Some beliefs are commonsense and therefore perfectly safe; many others are superstitious or just plain wrong. However, we typically do not question the accepted beliefs of the culture or group we move within. For instance, luck and random occurrences are concepts accepted in Western society, which mitigates against any suggestion that everything has a cause. We accept the idea of random events without thinking. On the other hand, we should not blindly accept causality simply because we have adopted a new belief system. We need to explore everything critically, taking our own experiences and inner life as material for investigation. The mind that weighs evidence and thinks rationally is our most important resource when dealing with this subject. If we adopt beliefs without investigation, our studies will become dry and tasteless.

A simple example that shows the ease with which we adopt beliefs is the way we so readily trust science. Nowadays scientific theories are very popular and we generally accept them, whether we really understand them or not. Currently conventional scientific opinion asserts that our mental life of thoughts, feelings, and sensations is nothing more than a product of chemical reactions within our brains and bodies. When these chemical reactions cease, according to these beliefs, the being also ceases. Of course this view that all mental activity is entirely dependent on the biological organism is not the only one currently espoused, but it seems to be the dominant one and one that many people accept without question. This kind of ignorance, I would say, is ignorance about the law of causality due to adopted beliefs or cultural conditioning, and is by no means an innate or natural ignorance.

Ancient or religious beliefs can also cause this kind of ignorance. Many people believe that we are created by God. I am not saying that this is necessarily wrong, but it does not hold true with the Buddhist idea of cause and effect. Out of this belief in God, many people have done amazing work, benefiting millions of people century after century. Nonetheless, the belief in a creator God goes against the concept of cause and effect and creates confusion about how things come into being. This is also an acquired ignorance.

Innate ignorance, in contrast, is not acquired from our environment but arises naturally for all sentient beings. Even without our culture causing us confusion, we would still be confused as a result of our innate ignorance. Innate ignorance is not dependent on reasoning. Spontaneously we feel that things and events, including our own existence, arise without depending on causes.

Thus, there is some kind of natural tendency to see things wrongly. I was brought up in a Buddhist family and studied in Buddhist schools and monasteries. Intellectually and quite rationally, I accept that I

had previous lives and that in those previous lives, causes and conditions were accumulated, and that this is the reason I now experience
things slightly differently from others. Rationally, I can think through
all these Buddhist beliefs, but inside, it does not always resonate with
my instinctive perception of how things occur.

For example, when we are facing difficulties we instinctively blame
someone else, seeing someone or something outside of us as responsi-
ble. The tendency to blame others is spontaneous. We do not have to
learn to do it. This is a kind of innate ignorance about the law of
causality.

AFFLICTIVE EMOTIONS

As a result of our fundamental confusion, an anxiety, no matter how
subtle, is created within us because we do not see the objects of our
perception correctly. This anxiety is a deluded or afflictive emotion.

Afflictive emotions arise due to the mind being either attracted
toward an object or repelled by it, so the two types of afflictive emotions are attraction and aversion. We should keep in mind that in
Buddhism these two terms have a wider significance than we normally
give them. When we use the term *attachment* in our day-to-day language, we are usually referring to a very gross level of attachment to
people or things. The terms as they are used here have a much deeper
and more subtle meaning. The mind, misconceiving the mode of existence of the object by seeing the object as existing from its own side,
instinctively either moves toward the object or away from it, depending on whether the object supports or threatens the mind's own sense
of a concrete, unitary self. We experience aversion toward something
that damages our sense of self, and attraction to something that bol-
sters our sense of self. This can be extremely subtle. Next time you
enter a crowded room, watch how you instinctively warm to certain

people and avoid others, even if you do so with no more than a flick of your eyes.

Root and secondary afflictive emotions

Attachment or aversion can either be a root afflictive emotion or it can manifest in the form of secondary afflictive emotions, so called because they arise only in certain specific circumstances. *Root afflictive emotion*, as the name implies, is the root cause of all the secondary afflictive emotions, which include pride, deluded doubt, and the various wrong views.

We all have emotions, but the term *afflictive emotions* suggests there must also be emotions that are *not* afflictive. When does a nonafflictive emotion become afflictive? From a Buddhist perspective, emotions that arise due to ignorance are those that, merely by their presence, immediately disturb the mind. Because there are different degrees of subtlety of ignorance, these emotions, too, range from gross to subtle, with subtle ignorance producing subtle afflictive emotions and gross ignorance producing gross afflictive emotions. The subtle emotions are very difficult to recognize as afflictive and are therefore more difficult to eliminate. However, any emotion that arises from a genuine feeling of compassion or love and is therefore not contaminated at all by ignorance is still an emotion, although not an afflictive one. We all have some degree of love and compassion, of course, but most of the time they are contaminated by our deluded minds.

THE THREE KINDS OF CRAVING

"Now this, bhikkhus, is the noble truth of the origin of suffering: it is this craving that leads to renewed existence, accompanied by delight and lust, seeking delight here and there; that is, *craving for sensual pleasures, craving for existence, craving for extermination.*"

In the sutra the Buddha lists three kinds of craving: craving for sensual pleasures, craving for existence, and craving for extermination. In the Tibetan Buddhist tradition, however, we study these three concepts in a slightly different order:

+ craving for sense pleasures
+ craving for transitory aggregates
+ craving for existence

Craving for sense pleasures

It is obvious that we crave sense pleasures, objects that bring some excitement or gratification to our sensory awareness. We sentient beings live in the so-called *desire realm,* where we are dominated by our five sensory consciousnesses and constantly in danger of being caught up in external objects. Our minds are continually attracted to the sights, sounds, and other sensations that comprise our experience, and when we are deprived of these things, our conceptual minds create objects internally with thoughts and memories. Particular sense attach-ments—such as the craving for delicious food or beautiful friends—might not be with us continuously; but in some form or another, even in sleep, our minds are forever chasing after things to please our senses.

If we examine this craving we will see that it is the spur that moti-vates so much of what we do in this life, and thus is the creator of so much stress and worry. Almost all the time, our search for the next gratifying thing is driving our behavior. The Pali term for craving sense pleasures, *kama tanha,* exemplifies this clearly—through our thirst (*tanha*) for sense pleasures (*kama*) we act, and because all of this arises from a deluded mind, the result is suffering.

Craving for transitory aggregates

It is interesting to examine craving for transitory aggregates in some detail, because the Mahayana and Theravada interpretations have some telling differences.

In Pali this craving is known as *vibhava tanha*, which is usually translated as "the thirst for nonexistence" or "self-annihilation." Ajahn Sumedho sees it as a desire to get rid of things, referring to things that we do not like.[16] Although both self-annihilation and aversion to things can be found in the Mahayana concept of this kind of craving, the Mahayana focuses to a greater extent on the vital last moments of this life, and calls this type of craving the *craving for transitory aggregates*.

This is a very important point. The craving for transitory aggregates can be attachment to our present healthy and beautiful aggregates, or, at a deeper level, it can also refer to the craving to get rid of these transitory aggregates when they not only no longer serve us, but are in fact a threat to our survival. Naturally we cling to our aggregates because they represent our entire existence, but a point comes in the death process when the end is inevitable and, due to our strong desire for existence, we desperately crave the next life and feel great aversion to the present aggregates because they are holding us back. This corresponds to the Theravada idea of the thirst for nonexistence.

Whereas Ajahn Sumedho's explanation of aversion to certain objects represents a view that considers the perspective of this lifetime alone, the Tibetan Buddhist explanation extends it to include aversion for our very aggregates at the time of death.

Craving for existence

In Tibetan Buddhist philosophy the third craving is a natural continuation of the second. This life is ending and the aggregates are dissolving, but our strongest and most subtle craving is for existence itself. Therefore, we release the life raft of this life and jump to the next.

The Tibetan explanation is very subtle, exploring the vital link between lives. As you will see when we look at the twelve links of dependent origination later, among the twelve links of the chain of cause and effect that keep us in samsara, the tenth is existence. This link is what we are talking about here. This craving makes the connection to the next life and determines what kind of experience we will have, so it is like a bridge from this life to the next.

The Tibetan Buddhist explanation is about becoming in terms of the next life, whereas equally validly Ajahn Sumedho describes it in terms of becoming within this life. He says:

> We get caught in that movement of striving to become happy, seeking to become wealthy; or we might attempt to make our life feel important by endeavoring to make the world right.[17]

When you think about it, the need for status or friends is a need to feel that we exist in some tangible way, so the explanations that the different traditions offer are not too disparate—both are a kind of craving for existence. The differences lie more in the subtle points than in the overall meaning. The Tibetan *see say* translates as *craving for samsara; see* comes from samsara (*see pa*) and *say* means desire or craving. Our strongest desire is the desire to exist. At death this desire manifests as the desperate craving to avoid annihilation and somehow jump to the next form of existence, and so we go from life to life and perpetuate cyclic existence. From the Tibetan Buddhist perspective, the previous craving, the craving for transitory aggregates, is the mind that desires the continuation of existence so badly that it rejects the current dying aggregates to jump to a new life. It is a rejection, an aversion, whereas this last one, craving for existence, is attraction. It is the actual jump.

Karmic Action

How Cause and Effect Works

Karma is such a complex and subtle subject that it is said that only buddhas understand its full implications, but knowing even a little about it can really change our relationship to people and things. Karma is a function of cause and effect.

Three conditions must be present for anything to come into being: the condition of the *existence of a cause*, the condition of *impermanence*, and the condition of *potentiality*.

Let us begin with the first, the condition of the existence of a cause. Things cannot come into being from nothing; everything that exists has been produced by something else. We see cause and effect in operation all the time in the natural world—we would never claim that an apple tree arose from nothing. What the Buddha did is simply extend our commonsense understanding of causality to encompass every aspect of reality, to both what is observable and what is not directly observable. The law of cause and effect is essentially a natural law. No other explanation makes rational sense.

The second condition that must be present is the condition of impermanence. Without the ability to change, nothing could create results. Permanence denotes an unchanging state. Something permanent cannot change from cause to result. Nor could it be part of a dynamic process that creates a result, since the act of creation itself changes the creator. Thus, there can be no permanent cause—in fact, in Buddhist logic, the term *permanent cause* is considered self-contradictory.

It is not sufficient for there to be a cause and for that cause to be impermanent. That impermanent cause must also have the third condition, potentiality—the potential to produce the corresponding result. An apple tree is a cause and is impermanent, but it does not have the potential to produce pineapples or other fruit. An apple tree can produce only apples. The potentiality must be concordant with the result. Using this type of logic, which systematically works through a seemingly obvious point that an apple tree cannot produce pineapples, we can then apply it to all cause and effect events.

SUBSTANTIAL AND CONTRIBUTORY CAUSES

The way causes produce results due to these three conditions is an important but only partial description of the matrix of events that make up the creation of any object or event. The entire picture is far more complex. Besides the material or substantial cause, many other contributing factors determine how something comes into being. These are *contributory causes* or *contributory conditions*, and together the substantial and contributory causes are often referred to as *causes and conditions*.

Although the substantial cause is also called the *material cause*, this does not mean that a physical or material substance must act as the main cause. This term *material* in this context simply means the essence of what transforms into the result. It can be physical, such as a seed that turns into a flower, but it can also be mental, such as a moment of anger that leads to vindictiveness.

Very often, the substantial cause alone is not enough to actually trigger the change. Water, moisture, warmth, and earth are all necessary to turn a seed into a flower. A dry seed sitting in a storeroom has the potential to produce a beautiful flower, but because it lacks the contributory causes, it will not produce the result. All the substantial and contributory causes must come together.

This process is the same for nonmaterial contributory causes. In order for a particular mental state to arise in our consciousness, there must be a substantial cause that is the main producer of that state. This is always the immediately preceding moment of mind. Then there are contributory causes, and these need not be mental. They might include a particular environment or an external event. When the substantial cause meets with the right contributory conditions, then the result can occur.

So this mechanism that brings about new things through causes and conditions always has both a substantial or main cause and a secondary or contributory cause. That is the case for all things. It is very important to understand this, because quite often when we are facing a situation, particularly a problem, we tend to get stuck on one single cause. We feel that *this* cause has produced this problem and that nothing can be changed. Looking at both the substantial and contributory causes together and knowing that it is a combination of both that has created the situation gives us a chance to explore more realistic ways to approach our problems.

We can take an employee who has been laid off as an example. Of course it is natural to feel depressed and think that nothing can be done. It is normal to see being laid off as the single cause of all the financial and psychological problems that ensue. If, on the other hand, the person can see how numerous conditions contributed to their current state, then that can defuse the obsession with the conceived "cause." If they can further see that in fact the main cause is far deeper, grounded in deep-rooted worries and insecurities rather than the external event that acted as a trigger, then there is a chance of changing the mental situation, if not the physical one. They may then be able to change the conditions that can be changed and not worry so much about those that cannot. Things naturally come into being from these two elements—substantial and contributory causes. When we examine our feelings, our experiences, our lives, and our karma, we will see how everything follows this same pattern.

KARMA

Without understanding that all things arise due to a substantial cause and secondary or contributory causes, it might appear that the theory of karma is something made up by Buddhists rather than simply the natural law of how things and events come into being. When we talk about karma, however, we go beyond the mere law of cause and effect. We look at how these causes and effects bring about happiness and suffering for ourselves and others.

Cause and effect is present in the natural world, but is it karma? Imagine that today is a beautiful day; the weather is nice, the sun is shining, the sky is clear. These factors all come into existence due to causes and conditions—the earth's movement around the sun, the wind, and the absence of clouds. But when we move into the realm of feelings, our happiness or unhappiness becomes involved. We might feel frustrated because the weather is beautiful and yet we are stuck in a stuffy office or, conversely, we might feel very happy because it is the weekend and we are enjoying the fine weather.

Karma enters the picture when our feelings become involved, when there is some volition or intention from our side. In fact karma brings happiness or suffering *because* of volition. With the movement of the earth or the absence of the clouds, generally there is no intention involved. All of this is natural. I say generally, because especially in the West you are very well versed in how our environment is affected by things like global warming, which has come about through our own decisions. But that is a separate point.

We become involved with a natural process through our volition—that is when happiness or suffering happens. It does not occur within the process itself. Whenever there is intention, karma is operating. *That* is the deciding factor. The mere existence of my present body has nothing to do with my karma. As we learn in biology, that mere existence is the continuation of molecules. But the moment my present body affects my feelings, there is karma. Then we can think in terms of the result of previous karma, or how we are creating new karma.

It is the same with our consciousness. Of the two types of phenomena, physical and mental, the mere continuation of the consciousness has nothing to do with karma. It is the natural law. But when that consciousness starts to feel that something is pleasant, unpleasant, or neutral—which when you think about it is all the time—then either karma starts to operate or the result of previously created karma starts to manifest. For example, if today I start to experience a very strong headache, from a Buddhist perspective there are definitely some causes. Because of some definite thing done in the past—the past karmic actions, the cause—there is now a headache, the result.

The mere continuation of our consciousness or of our physical body is exactly the same as the continuation of a flower. We cannot say that the flower has "the karma to be a flower." That is nonsense. When the consciousness reacts due to a coming together of conditions, karma starts to play a role. When I think about what a nice flower it is and I desire it, or when I am repulsed by its too-strong perfume, then there is a connection with my karma.

Buddhist literature, especially Mahayana, mentions two levels of karma: uncontaminated and contaminated. *Uncontaminated karma* refers to the karma of beings who are not necessarily enlightened but who have direct realizations of selflessness and emptiness. Their actions of body, speech, and mind are still considered karma, but they are uncontaminated because they are done within the direct realization of selflessness and so will never be the causes or conditions of rebirth in samsara. Furthermore, the karmic imprint left on the mindstream by such actions is also called *uncontaminated.*

When we talk about karma, however, we are almost always referring to the second type, *contaminated karma,* which is one of the main elements that bring about suffering. Until we realize emptiness directly, every karma, or action, that we create becomes either a main or secondary cause of rebirth in samsara. Therefore, this kind of karma is called *contaminated*. Even the minds of beings who have progressed far on the path and have many realizations, but have yet to directly realize ultimate truth, are always polluted by that ignorance. Consequently, all of the karma they create is created under its influence.

Karma is the cause, not the result

What is karma? When we Tibetans face difficulties, it is common to say, "Oh, it is karma," but this usually suggests some misunderstanding of karma. By labeling the difficulty itself as karma, we mistakenly equate karma with the result. One thing I want to make very clear is that *karma*, which is Sanskrit for action, is the *cause* and not the result.

When we create an action of body, speech, or mind, the conscious or subconscious volition that causes that action also creates a potential that is deposited in the mental continuum, the stream of consciousness. When the appropriate conditions arise, this potential becomes manifest as a positive or negative result. Again, it is the mental action itself that is karma, and not the ripening result.

In discussing karma, the Pali texts often use the term *volitional action*, which presents another picture of karma entirely. Volitional action is a culmination of ignorance and craving, and clearly implies the involvement of some kind of will. From ignorance and craving comes karma, or volitional action, which is enacted either mentally or physically.

The three stages of karma

A karmic act has three stages that determine whether it is complete or incomplete. The three stages are:

- ✦ intention
- ✦ action
- ✦ satisfaction

Sometimes a fourth category, that of the object itself, is also included.

Intention is the will, the wanting to do something—whether it is positive, negative, or neutral, and whether it is apparently operating or not. Without an intention, the mind does not move toward an action. After intention comes the *action* itself, which can be physical, verbal, or mental.

After we complete the action, we experience a sense of relief or *satisfaction*. Sometimes this is translated as *rejoicing*, but I prefer *satisfaction*. If within one volitional action all three aspects are present—the intention to do something, the actual action, and the sense of satisfaction at its completion—then from a Buddhist perspective it is a complete action.

We might think that most actions are incomplete because we so often seem to do things without intention. However, this would be misunderstanding what is meant by *intention* in this context. Intention does not just mean the motivations we are fully aware of. Intention can also refer to more unconscious drives, where we don't have to make any special effort to create them. Our motivations can arise spontaneously from unconscious concerns.

For example, if something is falling from a roof, our spontaneous reaction is to put up our hand to protect ourselves. This is a very unconscious action that comes from our deep, instinctive habit of self-preservation. Even though in our daily actions there may not be a deliberate intention by which we consciously choose our actions, on an unconscious and habitual level this is happening all the time.

It could be that we do an action accidentally and yet still experience a sense of satisfaction. We might mention something to someone we dislike that hurts them. It was not our conscious goal to do this, but, seeing their discomfort, we feel satisfied. Although the initial intention is missing, feeling is still part of both action and completion, and so it is still karma.

Furthermore, on another level, while we are committing that action there must be intention, because as long as consciousness is there, intention is present. According to Buddhism, as long as there is consciousness, at least six different types of minds are operating simultaneously, sometimes as many as thirty-two. One of these is intention. Because all of these minds occur concurrently, a deliberate sequence is not needed—for example, it is not necessary for intention to come first and action to come second. Intention is continually present during all activity, and because intention is present, we create karma.

If however, there is a clear sequence when we act—first intention, then action, then satisfaction—the result will be different from the result of an action with no definite sequence. If we steal on the spur of the moment, with no premeditated intention, the result will not be as heavy as it would be had we formed the intention in advance.

Consider two people, one with a disturbed mind and one whose mind is fairly normal. They both commit murder. Say the person with the disturbed mind does it as a spontaneous reaction while the other person plans it beforehand with strong intention. The result of these two karmic actions will be different because the intention is very different. For the former, a murder is still committed, but because one of the three stages is absent, the result won't be as heavy.

Similarly, if we sincerely regret a negative action rather than feeling satisfaction, the result will be less pronounced. This does not mean, however, merely mouthing words of regret. You can't cheat the law of karma like you can a human law.

Propelling and completing karma

Propelling or *throwing karma* is the karma that has the power to throw us into our future life. It is therefore very much connected to the third craving, the craving for existence. This craving is naturally very active just before our death when, consciously or subconsciously, we realize that this life is slipping out of our hands. However, this karma operates all the time, not only at that moment. Whether we cling to this life or the next life, we all have the same deep-rooted desire to exist. When our actions are motivated by that kind of desire, the action becomes propelling karma.

Completing karma is related to craving for sense pleasures, the first of the three cravings that is always present. Mere existence is never enough; within that existence we crave sensory objects to bring us pleasure, and that desire pushes us to act to accumulate more and more objects of desire.

It is often said that propelling karma is the karma that propels us into the next life, and completing karma is the karma that determines the kind of life we will experience. My feeling is that it is a little more complex than this, that both these desires—the craving for existence and the craving for sense pleasures—work together to bring about who we are. A human being is a complex aggregation of physical and mental constituents, and what we are—our propensities, affinities, irritations, traits, our whole personality in fact—comes about through a combination of these two different types of karma.

Karmic Imprints

The experience of pleasant or unpleasant things is not karma. Karma is the action that caused the experience. The imprint or propensity (Tib: *pak chak*) left on our mindstreams by that action has ripened due to causes and conditions coming together.

As I mentioned briefly, karmic imprints or propensities can be either uncontaminated or contaminated, but, it is almost always contaminated karmic imprints we discuss. In order to further our understanding of this subject we will examine how karmic imprints are created, where they are based, and what they are.

First, and this is vital, karmic imprints are created by mind and not by matter. Physically attacking or abusing someone does not create karmic imprints. However, the mind that motivates such actions *does* create karmic imprints. In this case, *mind* refers to one of the six consciousnesses—our five sensory consciousnesses and our mental consciousness.[18]

This does not mean that every instance of mental activity creates karmic imprints. Not every consciousness has that capacity, due either to the extreme brevity of the consciousness or its lack of clarity. If, for example, the eye consciousness makes contact with an object for a fraction of a second, it is probable that it will *apprehend*, but not *ascertain*, that object. This means that the image of the object will occur on the consciousness, but for too brief a time to be registered. In this case, it will not produce the propensity for the eye consciousness to have a similar type of experience in the future. In other words, no karmic imprint is created.

Similarly, the duration of a consciousness may be long, but due to the lack of clarity of that consciousness, no imprint is created. A person might be reading a book intently while a song is playing on the radio. Because the eye consciousness is the main focus, that person's ear consciousness apprehends the song, but the clarity of that consciousness is too weak to actually ascertain it. If someone asks them later whether a particular song was playing on the radio, they simply would not know. That ear consciousness in this instance, because of the lack of clarity, does not have the ability to create karmic imprints.

In general, however, when there is a consciousness with some force it creates a propensity either for a continuation of the same kind of consciousness or for some result to happen in the future. Although a physical or mental action may very well be associated with that consciousness, it is the mind that creates the karma and hence the karmic imprint.

Most Buddhist philosophical schools agree on the way that karmic imprints are created, but opinions differ about where they are based. Some scholars use the word *stored* for imprints, but I feel this gives some sort of sense that they are a physical entity. They are not physical entities, and there is no physical area where we might find them.

Our mental actions leave both long-term and short-term propensities on the mindstream. Most schools assert that long-term imprints are based only on the mental consciousness, which has the attribute of continuing day by day, year by year, and life by life, whereas short-term imprints can be based on the sense consciousnesses such as the eye and ear consciousness, and so forth.

It is asserted that although the sense consciousnesses cannot hold long-term propensities, they can produce consciousnesses of a similar sort. An eye consciousness apprehending a beautiful flower that causes us to have joy will create a propensity for a similar type of consciousness to arise in the future. This propensity does not last long, however, and will cease, because by nature sensory consciousnesses are unstable. When the base is lost, those propensities will also be lost. In other words, because the five physical sense consciousnesses depend on a physical body, when the physical sense powers disintegrate along with the disintegration of the physical body at the time of death, any remaining sense consciousness propensities with the five physical sense consciousnesses will also cease. This is not the case with the mental consciousness, which is not dependent on a gross physical body. Propensities created in the mental consciousness continue on after the death of the physical body.

Usually when we talk of karmic imprints, we are referring to those associated with the mental consciousness that goes from life to life and hence can hold long-term karmic imprints. The main criteria for being a base for karmic imprints is that the consciousness must be stable, continuing year by year and life by life, and by nature neutral—not positive, not negative, and not changing from one to the other.

It is a matter of dispute what kind of consciousness that is. Most schools assert that it is the very subtle mental consciousness, the deepest part of our minds, which goes from life to life. The fourth of the Buddhist philosophical schools, the Prasangika Madhyamaka (Middle Way Consequentialist), asserts that it is actually the mere "I" that is the base for karmic imprints. The Chittamatra school, however, asserts that a completely separate consciousness is the repository for the imprints, a consciousness they call the *mind basis of all.*

Finally, having understood how karmic imprints are created and where they are based, we need to know what they are. By definition, a karmic imprint is the potential produced by one of the six consciousnesses that, in the future, will bring about either its own continuation or one of the three types of result—a ripening result, an environmental result, or a result that is similar to the cause.

Basically what this means is that when a consciousness arises, it is energy, and as energy it has potential. This potential can be the potential to produce the continuation of the consciousness itself—one moment of eye consciousness naturally produces the potential for the next moment of eye consciousness, or the mind of love creates the energy for the mind of love to continue. It can also leave the seed for the future ripening of one of the three types of result mentioned above. For instance, the mind that creates the act of killing also creates the potential to experience the *ripening result* of being killed, the *environmental result* of rebirth in a barren place, or the *result that is similar to the cause,* in other words the propensity to kill again. In this way the cycle is perpetuated.

Another way to consider this is to look at the four main types of contaminated karmic imprints: the propensity of repetition, the propensity of the view of grasping at self, the propensity of samsaric experiences, and the propensity of similar factors.

The propensity of repetition is just that—the energy of a karmic action creates the potential for it to continue. One moment of anger has within it the seed to create another moment of anger. It is the fundamental nature of a mental action that it creates the energy to repeat itself.

The second, the propensity of the view of grasping at the self, refers to the mind that grasps at the five aggregates as the "I" or self. Every mental action is accompanied by this underlying sense of a real and solid "I." This perception contaminates even virtuous actions. This propensity carries within it the energy to repeat itself, and thus the view of an intrinsic "I" self-perpetuates.

The third, the propensity of samsaric experiences, refers to any kind of mind that we experience in connection with samsaric things. The mind attached to comfort or averse to discomfort, greedy for possessions or frightened of poverty—all of these keep us locked in samsara and carry within them the potential to produce similar minds. In particular, in the last moment of this life, we have a very strong mind that is terrified of extermination and thus leaps blindly to grasp at the next samsaric experience, the first moment of the next life.

The last type of contaminated karmic imprint, the propensity of similar factors, refers to the potential to experience a similar occurrence as a result. For example, the eye consciousness sees a beautiful or ugly thing and produces a propensity to experience a similar type of pleasant or unpleasant experience at some time in the future. Whereas the first propensity concerns immediate repetition in what could be described as a continuum, this one concerns the same kind of mind arising at some later time, when the causes and conditions come together.

Let us examine this debate: Are uncontaminated and contaminated karmic imprints innate—a natural part of our minds—or are they newly created, in other words, did they arise as the result of some past mental action? Within this debate there are three positions. Some Buddhist masters assert that all karmic imprints are innate; some insist that they are all newly created. Finally, some posit that certain types of karmic imprints are present within us by nature and certain types that are newly created. The position of the Gelug school, which is the Tibetan tradition I studied under, is the third.

Every school believes that enlightenment is possible, but the Gelug school asserts that the karmic imprints that make it possible for us to become enlightened have been with us forever. They are the very core of our being and are therefore innate. Similarly, in our unenlightened state it is possible to suffer, and that potential to suffer has also been with us since beginningless time. Therefore, this too is innate. As long as there is consciousness, these two potentials exist—the potential to become enlightened and the potential to suffer. They were not created from some previous consciousness and are therefore not newly created.

Beyond those two broad possibilities, however, the actual potential to create all the actions that will lead to our becoming enlightened or experiencing suffering, pain, and samsaric life *are* created within the framework of the consciousness. So, according to the Gelug tradition, certain levels of potential are naturally present and certain levels are newly created.

THE ORIGIN OF SUFFERING IS WITHIN SUFFERING ITSELF

Where does suffering come from? Investigating a problem we have, we might be able to identify a particular cause, but if we trace that back further we will inevitably find that the cause itself was the product of a deluded mind. We experience no suffering that is not caused by a deluded mind. If we could trace that deluded mind back, we would find that it arose because of another, deeper level of delusion in our mindstream. For instance, trouble at work might be caused by feelings of jealousy, which might in turn be caused by lack of self-worth, which in turn is due to not understanding the law of cause and effect. Further, that trouble will probably reinforce our lack of self-worth, which is the cause of more problems in the future. This is a vortex that causes us to descend more and more deeply into cyclic existence.

In fact, if we had the insight, we would undoubtedly come to the same conclusion that the Buddha came to—the origin of suffering arises from within suffering itself. They are not separate. Suffering and the origin of suffering depend on one another for their existence. Walpola Rahula says that this is one of the most important and essential points of the Buddha's teachings.[19]

For example, our aggregates in this life are the result of previous delusions and karma. Thus this present life is in the nature of suffering or dukkha. However our present life is not passive, it is active. Because it is under the power of delusion, it is the origin of suffering because it creates the causes that bring suffering results in either this or a future life. Therefore there is no clear-cut demarcation between the origin of suffering and suffering itself. In many cases, although they are cause and effect, they are co-existent.

Our present suffering is a result of previous suffering and it is also the cause of future suffering. As long as the deluded mind is present, there is no escape from this cycle. This is the key to understanding samsara.

Dealing with Afflictive Emotions

The truth of the origin of suffering consists of the relationship between ignorance, afflictive emotions, and karmic actions. Ignorance leads to afflictive emotions, which in turn cause karmic action to take place. Afflictive emotions and ignorance, as we have seen, are often lumped together under the heading of *delusions*. Of these two, afflictive emotions play the more important role in keeping us in this unenlightened state. They are of course connected, and when we try to eliminate one it always affects the other.

Generally speaking, afflictive emotions and thoughts are defined as those mental states whose mere occurrence creates an immediate disturbance within our minds. This disturbance is an affliction because it feels unpleasant, and it is a deluded mind because it does not accord with reality. All afflictive emotions are accompanied by a certain degree of misunderstanding of reality.

All Buddhist philosophical schools agree that negative states of mind like attachment, anger, or jealousy are misperceptions, but differences exist about what a misunderstanding of reality is. The Prasangika Madhyamaka school asserts some sorts of minds are afflictive emotions that the lower schools do not. One example is the key concept of self-lessness, in which the existence of a true, intrinsic "self" is refuted. The two lower schools believe that *something* is there, something intrinsically existent, because they believe that an ordinary being perceives things and events with a certain degree of validity. But the two upper schools say that no phenomenon exists truly; seeing things and events as existing from their own side is a wrong perception.

Suppose we are attracted to a beautiful flower. The two lower schools would say that an intrinsically existing beautiful flower does exist. They would posit that there is nothing wrong with the way our eye consciousness sees the flower—it is the attachment that is the afflictive emotion. In contrast, the two upper schools would say that there is something wrong with the actual perception of the flower. We will examine this further in the commentary on the last noble truth, the truth of the path, but I mention it now because in order to abandon afflictive emotions, we need to know how they arise within us.

Acquired and Innate Afflictive Emotions

Afflictive emotions can be acquired through the belief systems of our culture or through learning, or they can be innate. Unlike rationally arising afflictive emotions, which require effort to acquire, innate afflictive emotions arise unconsciously and exist without any apparent reason or effort. Of the two, acquired afflictive emotions are easier to eliminate.

If an afflictive emotion arises because of a cultural or philosophical view, then it is possible, by examining it rationally, to eliminate it. A very simple example is animal sacrifice. Even these days in India practitioners of some religions kill animals in sacrifice and offer the blood to their gods, believing that such things will bring wealth or fame or will please the gods, and that through this activity they will gain whatever they want. Those who hold such beliefs are influenced by the prevalent views of their culture. If they are able to rationally see that this kind of action, rather than increasing their happiness, in fact increases their suffering, they will stop engaging in such things, and the corresponding afflictive emotions will cease.

The direct way to eliminate such negative emotions, which are wrong conceptions based on misunderstandings, is to rationally explore the opposite way of thinking. When people see that killing animals is not the way to happiness, they let go of that view, and in that way the acquired afflictive emotion is comparatively easy to abandon.

Innate, or unconsciously arising, afflictive emotions are much more difficult to eliminate because they are caused by our innate ignorance and arise without reasoning or rational thought. Due to our previous lives' habits, beliefs, and actions, such afflictions arise in this lifetime without any other external influence, and become completely integrated with our thought processes.

Despite the difficulty of dealing with them, the process is exactly the same. First we must understand logically that something like attachment to pleasure is the cause of our suffering and not of our happiness. Then we must work to integrate that principle into our mindstreams.

As we discussed in the section on the first noble truth, the existence of all beings in an unenlightened state is a consequence of the dominion of afflictive emotions. As long as this remains so, complete happiness is impossible. Only when we really understand this cycle will we begin to see afflictive emotions as the real enemy, and as the source of all problems and difficulties.

Shantideva said that having afflictive emotions is like having a cobra coiled in our laps—as long as the cobra is there, there is no way to feel secure. I like this analogy. As someone who has seen a cobra, it really speaks to me. For unenlightened beings like us, from the second we wake up in the morning we are under the power of these afflictive emotions. As long as they are present, no real happiness or real freedom can arise. We need to be constantly aware how powerful afflictive emotions are and how much we live under their power.

Usually in our everyday life we think of *abandoning* in the physical sense, of throwing something away, but we abandon these afflictive emotions through constant awareness of what we are doing and the knowledge that as long as we are under their power there is no way to enjoy happiness. We need to see the afflictive emotions that completely ensnare us as something to be eliminated right now—just as we would abandon a snake in our laps.

Abandoning the unconsciously arising negative emotions, even in the form of potential, requires constant application of antidotes, such as meditating on emptiness. Only great consistency and power can eliminate these very subtle and deep-rooted propensities, which act as the origin of suffering.

THE TEN NONVIRTUOUS ACTIONS

Karmic actions are reactions to our afflictive emotions. Although it seems logical to think that we would eliminate our karmic actions by going after their causes, the afflictive emotions, this is not the way it works in practice. Afflictive emotions are so deep-seated and our habits so ingrained that it is hard to address them directly at first, so we start out by addressing our behavior. By reducing our negative karmic actions, we slowly reduce the hold our afflictive emotions have on us.

Karmic actions can be created only through what Buddhists call the three doors: the body, speech, and mind. As total beginners, we need to pay attention to the three doors, observing the kinds of actions that we do with our bodies, the conversations that we have in our daily interactions with people, and, of course, the thoughts that arise in our minds.

An obvious place to start in the process of abandoning negative karmic actions is by trying to avoid the ten nonvirtues. This seems very rudimentary, but it would be a huge mistake to think that avoiding the ten nonvirtuous actions is just an elementary practice. Maybe great practitioners can disregard them because virtue is second nature to them, but as beginners we really have to pay constant attention to them. Avoiding the ten nonvirtuous actions with the thought of attaining liberation or enlightenment is said to be the Buddhist way of engaging in their opposites—the ten virtuous actions. Of course it is a very positive thing to avoid killing and so forth, but when it is done with the motivation of attaining enlightenment, it becomes a very strong Dharma practice.

The ten nonvirtues are:

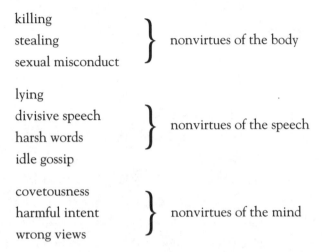

killing
stealing
sexual misconduct
} nonvirtues of the body

lying
divisive speech
harsh words
idle gossip
} nonvirtues of the speech

covetousness
harmful intent
wrong views
} nonvirtues of the mind

Killing is the greatest nonvirtue of all because taking another's life is the most harmful action that we can do. Although people might love their house or possessions, their lives are the most precious thing they have and the last thing they want to be separated from. However, it is not just humans that we should avoid killing, but all living beings—all beings with sentience and hence the basic ability to suffer. Although the majority of us would not consciously commit such a destructive action as murder, even harming another's body is a step in that direction, so we should abandon it entirely.

The second nonvirtue of the body is stealing. This refers to gross acts of stealing such as burglary and theft, but also includes any taking of something owned by someone else without permission. From that piece of chocolate cake that your roommate was keeping in the fridge to a floppy disc from the office—unless something has been offered to you in some way, it is considered stealing. In some way or other, taking what is not ours will definitely cause harm to others. The Buddha said that this applies to anything larger than a grain of rice, so we should all be very mindful not to commit this nonvirtue.

Sexual misconduct basically means hurting another through sex. Obviously, rape is a gross example of this, but from the sexual bullying of teenagers to the sexual politics of a marriage—from demanding sex out of anger to withholding sex in an effort to manipulate another— whenever we use sex or the threat of sex to harm someone else in some way, it is sexual misconduct. This is a huge cause of emotional damage in people's lives.

Among the nonvirtues relating to speech, telling lies is the first. Again we need to take this further than the overt act of saying something untrue. Lying is anything we say (or do not say) that is intended to deceive others. Remaining silent when talking would clarify a misapprehension is considered part of this nonvirtue.

Divisive speech is any verbal action that in any way causes friction between people. This can include deliberately setting out to break up a group or a partnership. In particular, splitting the Sangha is considered a very powerful nonvirtue. Divisive speech is usually much more subtle than that, however, such as the rumors someone might spread about a couple through jealousy.

Harsh words are obviously harmful, whether the harm is in the language itself or in the intent behind the words. And whereas the final nonvirtue of speech, idle gossip, might seem the least offensive, in some ways it is the most dangerous of all, because it is the one we tend to do the most often. Perhaps the words that we say are not directly harmful, but think of the hours we waste in meaningless chitchat, especially if we extend the definition of this nonvirtue to include watching soap operas!

The final "door" through which we commit negative actions is the mind, and of course this is the most harmful of all of them, because it is the mind that motivates all other actions. Covetousness and harmful intent may or may not lead to physically harming another person, but they surely will harm ourselves.

Wrong view, the last nonvirtue, is the greatest danger because all other nonvirtues spring from this. Generally, wrong view means to deny such basic truths such as the law of cause and effect. Of course, we all believe in the law of cause and effect, but, if we are really honest with ourselves, we do not often act as if we do. If simply *knowing* that a certain action will cause us suffering in the future meant that we would never do that action again, then we would immediately stop committing any of these ten nonvirtues.

Dealing with the Coarsest First

We must therefore pay attention to the three doors of body, speech, and mind in our everyday lives in order to reduce nonvirtues and address our karmic actions. We need to play with our thoughts—trick them a little if necessary. This is like people who want to give up their nicotine addiction by wearing a patch. If it works it does not really matter whether the chemical in the patch is effective or whether it is just a placebo to help the mind. Sometimes we need to cheat our thoughts, because reducing the negative karmic actions is the only chance we have to deal with our afflictive emotions.

We ultimately need to cut the root of our suffering, our basic ignorance, but it is unrealistic to think that we can go straight to the root. There is a definite sequence to freeing ourselves from suffering. In *Four Hundred Stanzas (Chatuhshataka)*, Aryadeva makes the point that we must deal with the coarsest levels first, dealing consciously and determinedly with the negative habit that most plagues us. If it is jealousy, then jealousy is what we must strive to lessen and eliminate. The more subtle afflictions will come to light only after we have begun to subdue the grosser ones.

When I was in Sera Monastery we had to cut down a very old banyan tree in order to build our debating yard. A banyan's branches grow down and become roots, and banyan trees can be enormous. In South India, in fact, there is a famous tourist spot where one tree covers ten acres. The younger monks with the big muscles thought the first thing to do was to cut the main trunk, but the elder monks said that this was not the best way to cut it down because it had so many branches and it could damage other things. Their method was to cut the branches first, to make it smaller, and then move on to the main trunk.

We were studying afflictive emotions at that time, and a monk three years older than I argued to cut the trunk of the tree straight away. One of the more senior monks told him that his debating did not go with his actions. Like the tree, in dealing with the mind we need to go from the coarsest to the subtle, step by step. In that way both the origin of afflictive emotions and the origin of karmic actions can be abandoned.

Just understanding how harmful smoking is probably will not break the habit—this is something we might have to slowly cut back on. Similarly, a person who easily gets angry might well know how harmful it is but for a long time will probably have to determinedly stop doing the harmful action connected with anger while the angry mind continues. First the manifestation of anger is abandoned, and then the anger itself. It still goes from coarsest to subtle.

For someone wanting to abandon the truth of the origin of suffering, the initial importance is the first aspect, the origin of karmic actions. Understanding the importance of effort and constantly working to reduce unskillful actions will help us to reduce our negativities. In contrast, trying to get at the root while completely indulging in negative actions just does not work.

The Wheel of Life

The Twelve Links of Dependent Origination

We can understand how the truth of the origin of suffering works to produce the truth of suffering through the teaching called the *twelve links of dependent origination*. This teaching explains the mechanism that produces the two sets of cause and effect (suffering and origin, cessation and path).

The twelve links are links in a chain, a closed circle, which represents cyclic existence. This is symbolized in the traditional illustration of the wheel of life. Here you see the six realms of existence determined by the three poisons at the hub of the wheel: the pig representing ignorance, the cock desire, and the snake aversion. The rim of the wheel shows the twelve links, starting with the blind man (representing ignorance) at the top and moving clockwise around to the last link, the corpse (representing aging and death). All this is held in the jaws and claws of Yama, the Lord of Death.

Our fundamental ignorance produces the volition to act (karma) that becomes the cause for suffering. A causal state produces a resultant state, which itself is a cause that produces a result—and so it goes on endlessly. The teachings on the twelve links are very helpful to help us clearly understand how we are circling in endless suffering. As long as we are under the power of karma and delusions in this process, there is no end to the cycle.

The twelve links of dependent origination (with their representations in the wheel of life) are:

+ ignorance (a blind person)
+ karma (a potter)
+ consciousness (a monkey)
+ name and form (people in a boat)
+ sense bases (an empty house with six windows and a door)

- ✦ contact (a couple in sexual union)
- ✦ feeling (a hunter with an arrow in his eye)
- ✦ clinging (a drunkard)
- ✦ craving (a monkey reaching for fruit)
- ✦ existence (a pregnant woman)
- ✦ birth (a woman giving birth)
- ✦ aging and death (a corpse)

In order to understand how the first set of cause and effect—suffering and origin—works, we examine the twelve links in forward order, seeing how the first link (ignorance) leads to the second (karma), and so on up to the twelfth (aging and death). Then to understand the second set—cessation and path—and how the truth of the path cuts cyclic existence and so is the cause of cessation, we can actually reverse the order of the twelve links, putting the last link (aging and death) first. If we do not want aging and death, we need to eliminate the eleventh link (birth), and in order to do that we need to eliminate the tenth (existence), and so on.

How the Twelve Links Operate over Three Lifetimes

The *Rice Seedling Sutra*, in which the Buddha teaches about dependent origination, says:

> Due to existence of this, that arises.
> Due to the production of this, that is produced.
> It is thus, due to ignorance, there is compositional action;
> Due to compositional action, there is consciousness.

Although a major topic on its own, the twelve links of dependent origination can also be studied as an expansion of the explanation of

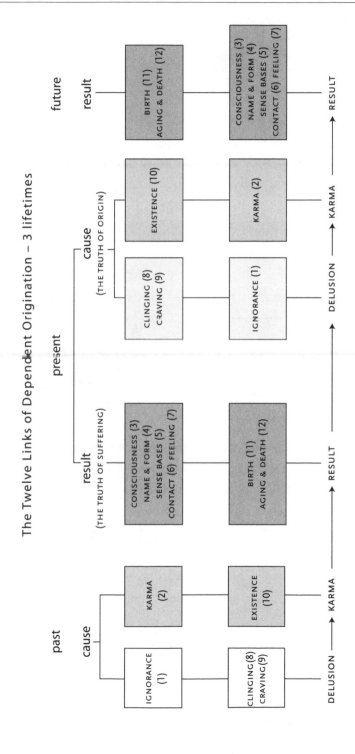

The Twelve Links of Dependent Origination – 3 lifetimes

the first two noble truths. This teaching can be understood from two perspectives—showing how the first and second noble truths are connected, and showing how the whole of cyclic existence functions because of those first two noble truths. For our purposes we will very briefly consider the chart on page 95 to see how the twelve links connect our past, present, and future lives.

First we will look at the middle section, our present life, in which you can see six boxes that contain all twelve links. These are divided into two—the two boxes on the left labeled "result" and the four on the right labeled "cause." Thus all these twelve links exist in our present lives as either result or cause.

Starting from the bottom middle box, the first link is *ignorance* (1). From ignorance we move to the box on the right, *karma* (2). These two operate to create *clinging and craving* (8 and 9), in the middle top box. After that comes *existence* (10), in the top right-hand box.

The two middle boxes, *ignorance* and *clinging and craving*, are part of "delusion," whereas the boxes on the right, *karma* and *existence*, are under the subtitle "karma," showing that delusions and karma are their causes.

Although we can experience some results of these two causes within this lifetime, the main result will ripen in our future lives. The right-hand section of the chart titled "future" includes two boxes: *birth* (11) and *aging and death* (12); and *consciousness* (3), *name and form* (4), *sense bases* (5), *contact* (6), and *feeling* (7). So moving from *ignorance* in the middle section, "present," into the "future" section, you can see one complete set of the twelve links of dependent origination.

Coming back to the present, under "result," there is *consciousness* (3), *name and form* (4), *sense bases* (5), *contact* (6), and *feeling* (7), and then *birth* (11) and *aging and death* (12). These are the result of the past lifetime, and under the heading of "past" is a complete set of "delusion" (*ignorance* and *craving and clinging*) and "karma" (*existence* and *karma*). So again, the links under "result" in the present when combined with the links under "past" from our past lives make a complete set of the twelve links.

This is how the twelve links operate in our existence. Although all twelve links are operating in this present life, they do so in different ways—some as a result of our previous lives' delusions and karma, and some as the causes for future lives' links of birth, aging and death, and so forth. Although the chart might seem a bit confusing at first, I think it is very important to study it and really get a feeling for how the twelve links are connected over subsequent lives.

THE TWELVE LINKS IN FORWARD ORDER

Taking the middle section of the chart, "present," we now look at the twelve links in forward order.

1. ignorance

In the lower middle box, *ignorance* comes under the heading "cause." There are many different levels of ignorance, but here we are referring to ignorance of the more subtle levels of cause and effect and to the ignorance of the view of selflessness.

2. karma

The second link, in the right lower box next to ignorance, is *karma* or volitional action. We have previously covered karma, so there is no need to go into detail here. However, among the two types of karma—contaminated and uncontaminated—this refers strictly to contaminated karma.

3. consciousness

Following the normal order of the twelve links of dependent origination, the next is the top box of the present life's "result" column, where the third link is *consciousness*. Here again, there are different types of consciousness, and this refers mainly to the subtle levels of consciousness that act as a bridge from this life to the next.

4. name and form

Name and form refers to conception, when the individual's consciousness enters the womb, after which form starts to develop. *Name* refers to the moment we are conceived and the aggregates of our next life start to develop. Some types of being do not have the aggregate of form, so for them at this point only the four mental aggregates start developing, hence the division between the two aspects of this link.

5. sense bases

This is also sometimes translated as *six sense spheres*. In other words, this is the development of our sensory consciousnesses.

6. contact

After developing our sensory consciousnesses, there is *contact* with sensory or mental objects.

7. feeling

In this life, as soon as we develop into body and form aggregates and our sensory consciousness makes contact with an object, we begin to experience *feeling*—positive, negative, or neutral.

8. clinging

The eighth link, *clinging*, in the top middle box, can also be called *attachment*. You should use whichever word makes more sense to you. This refers to a strengthening of the previous link, feeling, when the mind actually moves toward an object with either attachment or aversion.

9. craving

The ninth link is *craving* or *grasping*. The clinging we feel for an object can become very strong, and this marks the point when the mind does more than move toward the object—it actually wants to possess the object in some sense. This is called craving. These two links are differentiated by degrees of intensity, and the ninth link represents the greater degree.

10. existence

The tenth link, *existence* or *becoming*, is the top right box. At the moment of our death when the previous link of craving or grasping becomes very intense, it moves into the tenth link of existence, close to bringing the result of the next life.

11. birth

Now we progress into the next section, "future." The top link in the top box is *birth*. Strong craving becomes existence, which creates the result of birth.

12. aging and death

Immediately after birth, *aging* begins, which leads ultimately to *death*. Therefore, aging and death are included in one link.

This process really just looks at one cycle of the twelve links of dependent origination. In terms of considering how this works according to cause and effect, we should begin at the middle of the "present" section under "causes" and move to the future. Then we will see that the order is very logical and precise.

The Four Characteristics of the Truth of Origin

Each noble truth can be explained by way of its four unique characteristics. For the truth of the origin of suffering they are:

+ causes
+ origin
+ strong production
+ condition

These four characteristics explain the origin of our suffering by showing how karma and delusions act together to bring it about. The first characteristic, *causes*, refers to the fact that contaminated karma and delusions are constantly arising within our mental continuums, and because of their nature they have the quality of being the causes of suffering. We need to clearly understand this.

Many causes and conditions make up and determine our existence, but this second noble truth points to the fundamental cause. The second characteristic, *origin*, indicates that afflictive emotions and contaminated karma are the actual origin of suffering, not just intermediate links in a chain of cause and effect. They have the characteristic of being the origin of suffering.

The third characteristic is *strong production*, meaning that delusions and karma are more than just passive ingredients in the creation of suffering; they act forcefully as its main causes. And finally the fourth characteristic, *condition*, adds to this, indicating that karma and delusions are more than just the main causes of suffering, they are the contributory causes as well. In other words, they are the whole business—the entire reason we suffer.

4 THE TRUTH OF CESSATION

Cessation, Liberation, and Enlightenment

THE THREE PHASES

"Now this, bhikkhus, is the noble truth of the cessation of suffering: it is the remainderless fading away and cessation of that same craving, the giving up and relinquishing of it, freedom from it, nonreliance on it...

"'This noble truth of the cessation of suffering is to be realized': thus, bhikkhus, in regard to things unheard before, there arose in me vision, knowledge, wisdom, true knowledge, and light.

"'This noble truth of the cessation of suffering has been realized': thus, bhikkhus, in regard to things unheard before, there arose in me vision, knowledge, wisdom, true knowledge, and light."

As with the first two noble truths, the third noble truth has three phases. The first phase describes the nature of the truth of cessation, the second phase explains what should be done by the practitioner with regard to the truth of cessation, and the third phase explains the ultimate result or complete attainment when the practitioner has managed to realize that cessation.

In the first phase, when the Buddha explains the nature of the truth of the cessation of suffering, he says it is "the remainderless fading away and cessation of the same craving." This cessation is the complete cessation, so that nothing remains, of the previous two noble truths—suffering and its origin. This is what is meant by the "same" craving—craving that is one of the main causes of suffering. This is not just any cessation; it is the cessation in our everyday lives, in our everyday minds, of all our fears, and all those deluded minds we have already discussed. When the presence of these mental states within our mindstreams is eradicated, that is the cessation of suffering and its origin.

In the second phase, the noble truth of the cessation of suffering is to be "realized," which means actually achieving the utter end of suffering and its origin within the mindstream. Once the practitioner realizes the cessation of suffering and its origin, this cessation never deteriorates. Sufferings that were previously experienced will not be re-experienced. Realized once, this cessation is the final realization, attainment, and result. This is the third phase.

What Is the Cessation of Suffering?

While exploring the third noble truth, the truth of cessation, a lot of the ideas might seem very intellectual, so it is always good to remind ourselves that the purpose of study is only to enhance our understanding of how things actually function in our daily lives, and thereby develop ourselves so that we become more gentle, caring, and sincere. Intellectualizing alone is dry and worthless. Only by enhancing the positive qualities of the good heart and understanding the nature of reality can we reduce the emotions that bring problems and difficulties, and slowly subdue the mind.

Cessation, as the name implies, is related to stopping—it is the complete end of all our suffering through relinquishing it, as the sutra says, until it fades into nothing and no suffering remains. We will know freedom only after we abandon our reliance on this samsara that we see as happiness but which in fact is nothing but suffering.

The annihilation of the craving that keeps us clinging to cyclic existence is, at its very deepest level, the annihilation of our misconceptions about reality. This is only implicit within the sutra. We are bound to cyclic existence by the ignorance that actively fails to understand the nature of reality and that everything is interdependent and lacks any sense of intrinsic, independent reality.

In trying to understand such a subtle concept as well as to express it, different traditions have used different terms and approached it from different angles. Whereas Walpola Rahula uses terms such as absolute truth or ultimate reality, Mahayana scholars such as His Holiness the Dalai Lama quite often use emptiness or ultimate truth. Although referring to the same thing, each term gives a slightly different flavor, and so it is very useful to analyze them and see the subtle variations in the approach used by different scholars.

Rahula, approaching this from the perspective of Theravada, says that the cessation of suffering is the emancipation from suffering, from the continuity of dukkha, and is *nibbana* (Skt: *nirvana*).[20] This, he says, is the real nature of absolute truth or ultimate reality—it is not some physical state we enter when we are finally liberated from our delusions.

When His Holiness the Dalai Lama talks of cessation he is even more explicit:

> As Nagarjuna says, a true understanding of liberation should be based on an understanding of emptiness, because liberation is nothing other than the total elimination, or total cessation, of delusion and suffering through insight into emptiness. The

concept of liberation is therefore very closely related to that of emptiness, and just as emptiness can be inferred, so can moksha [liberation].[21]

Not only are emptiness and liberation almost identical, but according to His Holiness they can both be understood through reason, making our intellectual understanding an invaluable tool to gain access to the states of mind that will ultimately liberate us.

SYMBOLIC, RESIDUAL, AND NONRESIDUAL CESSATION

Liberation, cessation, and nirvana are synonyms, although there are many different types of cessation. Although some traditional texts cite twenty different types, the most important division is that division between the cessation of the obscurations to liberation and the cessation of the obscurations to enlightenment, which will be discussed later. These two categories of cessation both have different levels, usually divided into three:

+ symbolic cessation
+ residual cessation
+ nonresidual cessation

Symbolic cessation

Symbolic cessation is sometimes called *temporary cessation* because its experience can be reversed. Symbolic cessation simply refers to the temporary stopping of a negative mind—such as when we actively work on our anger until we manage to overcome it. The anger has stopped, but if we then discontinue whatever technique we were using to deal with it, when the right circumstances arise, the anger will probably arise again. Thus, this state is a cessation in that something has ceased, but it is symbolic or temporary because the root cause has not been destroyed and the afflictive emotion can occur again. It is not a complete cessation of that deluded mind.

Traditionally it is said that through single-pointed meditation, we can temporarily experience complete calm, withdrawing all of our sense consciousnesses from sensory objects so that we experience no distraction from external phenomena. This is symbolic or temporary cessation. The mind has withdrawn from the external object but has not really dealt with the root of the problem. There is some kind of cessation, and as long as we are in that state we feel serene, but that state is not everlasting cessation. As soon as our minds begin to relate with external objects again, we lose that serenity.

Certain practitioners can keep that state of mind right up until death, completely withdrawing their sense consciousnesses from external objects and experiencing total internal peace. However, when they begin a new life, all their new sensory consciousnesses will start seeking external objects. So again, this is a symbolic or temporary cessation because it is not permanent.

His Holiness the Dalai Lama says that we should not accept that liberation is possible simply because it is stated in the scriptures, and I think that this is where contemplating symbolic cessation can be very helpful. If we look at the ways we can reduce or even stop our anger, even for a short time, we will see that we can definitely experience some degree of cessation. On this basis, through reason, we can infer that complete cessation is also possible.

The texts state that there are four steps to achieving complete cessation: seeing that delusions and suffering are impermanent, seeing that there are methods to deal with them, seeing that these methods are available to us, and seeing that we ourselves can apply these methods.

Our goal, which is to eliminate all delusions and suffering from our mindstreams, would be impossible to achieve if these things were permanent and unchanging. Therefore the first step in freeing ourselves is to really understand that delusions and suffering are in fact impermanent, and hence changeable. Because this is so, it is possible to reduce them and eventually eliminate them completely.

If it is theoretically possible to deal with our afflictive emotions, the second step then is to investigate whether there are any actual methods, traditionally called *antidotes*, that could be used to accomplish this. Having established them, we should try to discover if these methods are available to us, and then move on to seeing that we ourselves can actually use them.

These four steps are very skillful, in that they lead us from an intellectual understanding of the possibility of liberation or enlightenment to a conviction that this is something we can actually pursue. This relentlessly rational step-by-step explanation of how to gain freedom sounds very intellectual, but it is in fact a great inspiration to see that we can actually do it.

In order to really appreciate that we are capable of complete cessation, we need to be aware that in general we as humans are much more capable than other beings, mentally and physically. Not only do we have incredible potential because of the physical and mental aggregates that we have gained in this human existence, but we also have the capacity to transcend our suffering. We can recognize that delusions such as craving and confusion are not in any way inseparable from our minds. Whether this is a realizable fact or merely religious dogma is something we really need to investigate, as it is crucial to understanding the route out of suffering.

We are dealing here with a process. Complete cessation is the end product of working through many temporary cessations, and while it is important to always have the end product in mind, it is equally important to be realistic in our expectations. In Mahayana Buddhism in particular we recite the phrase "all sentient beings" many times a day. Everything we do is for (or should be for) the benefit of all sentient beings. Because of who we are and the society we live in, we then feel guilty because we are not focused on all sentient beings and not doing enough for their complete enlightenment.

I find that frustration understandable but based on unrealistic expectations; it is too ambitious, and it may not even be what the Buddha meant by benefiting all sentient beings. If we manage to benefit even one sentient being with a pure heart, I think that is enough. Of course two or three is better, but we need to let go of the unrealistic expectation of being able to save every single being this instant. That is a wonderful aspiration, but as an immediate goal it is naively idealistic.

In reality cessation is a slow process. We need to work on diminishing our delusions, working on the strongest first, and slowly moving toward temporarily stopping them and then eliminating them completely. Whether anger, jealousy, attachment, or pride—whatever our strongest delusions are—we need to wholeheartedly put effort into eliminating them and then progress to the subtler delusions.

This is where real practice begins. Although we are talking about the complete cessation of all delusions, as I have mentioned, the starting point is to concentrate on our strongest delusion, such as anger, and apply the four steps. Through using the different methods and approaches, we will hopefully find that our anger has diminished, without in any way diminishing our minds. This is the sign that mind and anger can be separated, because if anger and mind were inseparable, when anger diminished and stopped, so, too, would mind.

We can experience a wonderful freeing and lightening of the mind by observing this process and actually realizing that it applies not just to one negative emotion in a partial, temporary way, but to all negative emotions in a total, permanent way. It is just a matter of time and practice. In this way I find the understanding of symbolic cessation to be crucial in understanding real cessation.

Residual cessation

Both the Theravada and Mahayana traditions agree that a human being with a physical body can achieve complete cessation. Through systematic reduction of our delusions we can finally completely eliminate them, but if we manage to do it in this lifetime we are still left with this physical body that has been produced by our previous lives' delusions and karma. The mind is cleansed of all delusions, but the body is still subject to the sufferings inherent in its nature.

This cessation is called *residual cessation*. It means that the cessation happens within the container of the body, which is still the result of delusions and karma, and that therefore, although mental cessation has been achieved, a residue of karma will not disappear until the body ceases.

Nonresidual cessation

Once the person dies, however, and the body with its "residual" delusions and karma ceases, this cessation becomes pure cessation in that nothing of delusions or karma remains in any way in that person's continuum. That is called *nonresidual cessation*.

While the person is alive in that particular body, the residue must remain, because the body was caused by delusions and karma and hence is bound to old age, sickness, and death. Even the Buddha was subject to those things. The demarcation is when that person dies and the body ceases—at that point the cessation becomes nonresidual.

The Theravada and Mahayana traditions actually have very different theories on this point. In the Theravada tradition, when a person achieves nonresidual cessation or liberation, everything ceases—not only their physical body and the other aggregates, but also the subtle mental continuation of the person. The Mahayana tradition sees this differently, asserting that once a person achieves individual liberation as an arhat, their mental continuum does not stop after death.

According to them, it is the continuation of samsara and delusion that is stopped, not the individual. Wherever that being takes rebirth, he or she may remain for a very long duration, even eons, in a meditative state, rather than in an active role benefiting other sentient beings—but the mind nonetheless continues.

LIBERATION AND ENLIGHTENMENT

For the Theravada practitioner, the primary aspiration is to be free from this conditioned existence, to achieve liberation. Hence this path is called the *individual liberation vehicle*. For the Mahayana practitioner, the goal is to free all others, and in order to do this the practitioner must attain enlightenment for him or herself. Just as there are two different goals, there are two different initial aspirations and two different methods to achieve these goals. This is the core of the differences between the two traditions.

A thorough understanding of the way the twelve links bind us to this endless cycle of suffering could be quite depressing, but it provides an incentive to sincerely look for a way out. Hence, for the Theravada practitioner, the driving force behind such a practice is the sincere wish to be free. A practice becomes a Mahayana practice when that wish is taken a bit further. The Mahayana practitioner sees how the twelve links imprison him or her, and then sees further that this is true for all beings. Just as the thought of the practitioner's own endless suffering is unbearable, so too is the thought that all beings are enduring the same endless suffering. Therefore the aspiration is not to free oneself alone, but to work toward all beings becoming free. With that kind of aspiration the practitioner begins to practice.

Mahayana texts state that all beings will eventually go on to attain enlightenment, and therefore even practitioners of the individual

liberation vehicle will sooner or later go beyond liberation to eliminate the obscurations to knowledge and become fully enlightened
beings. This is, of course, strongly debated, and I cannot myself say
whether this is true—but to me it makes sense.

In the Mahayana tradition, the difference between liberation and
enlightenment is very clear-cut, but the Theravada texts tend to dis-
agree, positing either that a practitioner who has achieved liberation
will not necessarily go on to achieve enlightenment, or that liberation
and enlightenment are the same thing. According to Mahayana texts,
even after liberation the continuum of an individual liberation practitioner will continue. However, because that mind is in perfect peace,
there are no senses or feelings to stimulate it, and in order to pursue
enlightenment there must be compassion, which is a feeling.
Therefore, this practitioner might remain in that state for eons before
something happens to trigger the wish to move on. These arguments
are very Mahayana-based, and I have heard them since I was eighteen,
so they tend to be things I just accept, although I really don't know if
this is actually the case.

Whether or not the end product is the same, at the initial stage of
practice there is definitely a difference. This leads me to believe that
because of having initially different motivations, which subsequently
trigger different actions, the result must also be different in some way.
Just looking at what we beginners do on a daily basis shows this clearly.
If we are following a Mahayana practice, the emphasis is very much on
doing things for all sentient beings. If we follow a Theravada tradition,
there is no such emphasis. That is not to say that a Mahayana practitioner has compassion whereas a Theravada practitioner does not—it's
just that one practitioner works toward enlightenment in order to free
others whereas the other's emphasis is on individual liberation.

However, on both paths we need to interact with others. To
progress toward liberation, we need to practice patience, which is

impossible without others. We need to address our own anger, which arises only from working with others, and of course to develop love we must be in contact with beings in relation to whom we can express it. So the difference in the paths is not that one nurtures the welfare of others and the other neglects it, but that the emphasis of the motivation of each is different. It is definitely not the case that Theravada practitioners are selfish and Mahayana practitioners are selfless.

None of us has yet lost our sense of self, so in a way we are all selfish, but the selfish mind can be positive or negative. The negative selfish mind wants things purely for its own satisfaction and neglects others' rights and happiness, whereas the positive selfish mind uses that strong sense of self-concern to help others. Without self-worth, I do not think we can do anything for others, so it is not necessary to destroy ourselves to achieve liberation. However, the negative selfish mind *must* be destroyed.

Cessation and Enlightenment

Cessation According to Theravada

Both the Theravada and Mahayana traditions completely accept that within this body, which is the result of delusions and karma, we can completely realize nirvana. In the Theravada tradition, however, ultimate reality or absolute truth seem to mean that the individual person is completely free from delusions and karma and, once the current rebirth ends, will never take another. This is ultimate reality in the sense that the person will never return to this circle of rebirth, aging, and death, and it is absolute truth because nirvana has been achieved. Nirvana is seen as an ultimate, an end, and as such is inexpressible. Walpola Rahula says:

People often ask: What is there after Nirvana? This question cannot arise because Nirvana is the Ultimate Truth. If it is Ultimate, there can be nothing after it. If there is anything after Nirvana then that will be the Ultimate Truth and not Nirvana. A monk named Radha put this question to Buddha in a different form: "For what purpose (or end) is Nirvana?" This question presupposes something after Nirvana when it postulates some purpose or end for it. So the Buddha answered: "O Radha, this question could not catch its limit" (i.e., it is beside the point). One lives the holy life with Nirvana as its final plunge (into the Absolute Truth), as its goal, as its ultimate end.[22]

Rahula suggests that nirvana is no longer existence as we know it—it is not a realm that a buddha enters, and says that the phrase "entered into nirvana" does not exist in the sutras. The only closely related Pali phrase is *parinibutto* (Skt: *parinirvana*), which denotes that the buddha or arhat has no further existence after death. So in the Theravada tradition, the individual person who realizes nirvana or ultimate reality is free from delusions and karma and will not take further rebirths.

When Mahayana texts use terms such as *nirvana* or *cessation*, they are referring to emptiness (and here I am talking about the view of the highest philosophical school, the Prasangika Madhyamaka). For them, cessation is ultimate truth. They do not accept ultimate truth in the Theravada sense of freedom from rebirth, but rather as the direct realization of the absence of inherent existence of all phenomena.

The Two Obscurations

	individual liberation vehicle	universal liberation vehicle
to be overcome	obscurations of defilements	obscurations of defilements and obscurations of knowledge
goal	liberation	enlightenment

Through spiritual development, suffering slowly diminishes and the various cessations begin to emerge. There are two main types of cessation, which have either liberation or enlightenment as their ultimate goal. To achieve them we need to overcome two types of obscurations:

+ obscurations of defilements
+ obscurations of knowledge

To achieve liberation, practitioners need to overcome all the obstacles that block them from realizing selflessness and from eliminating all negative states of mind. These obstacles are called the *obscurations of defilements*. Once liberation is achieved, subtle stains remain on the consciousness—a residue of wrong views. To continue on the path and achieve enlightenment, the *obscurations to knowledge* must also be overcome. In this way, liberation and enlightenment are different—in terms of the methods that are used to achieve them and in terms of the specific obscurations that block the goal. Enlightenment requires that extra step.

Although these seem to be two different obstructions to two different goals, this does not mean that a person on the path to enlightenment has only to contend with the second set of obscurations.

Practitioners on this path must eliminate both. The obscurations of defilements are related to our emotional tendencies, and so when we work on lessening our anger, attachment, jealousy, and so forth, we are working with our obscurations of defilements. The obscurations of knowledge are the very subtle obscurations, such as the propensities for misconceptions of reality. To a certain degree these still remain in the minds of those who have achieved liberation through following the first path.

If that is so, then what is liberation? In this sense liberation means liberation from samsara, from taking rebirth due to delusions and karma. Having achieved that state, although a person might then be free from the obscurations of defilements and therefore no longer a samsaric being, according to Mahayana that person is not a buddha. Nor is he or she a god or a being of the formless realm, because those realms are still in samsara. One who has attained freedom from the obscurations of defilements is called an *arhat*. To be a buddha, the individual must be completely free from the obscurations of knowledge.

Again, each of these two obscurations has two levels—those acquired through learning and innate obscurations. The Mahayana literature in particular presents many methods for dealing with these two levels of obscurations.

THE TWO CESSATIONS

Of the Indian philosophical schools considered important by Tibetan Buddhism—Vaibhashika, Sautrantika, Chittamatra, and Madhyamaka— all four accept two different types of cessation that arise when the two types of obscurations are ceased: liberation from samsara and full enlightenment.

It may seem quite academic, but understanding the differences among the schools can actually be quite illuminating. The first two schools, on the one hand, believe that certain beings will never progress past the first cessation, and hence will never achieve enlightenment. The two higher schools, on the other hand, also accept two cessations, but assert that all living beings will eventually attain the second cessation, full enlightenment.

It is possible for the first cessation, liberation from samsara, to be obtained while the practitioner still possesses the contaminated body aggregate. This is called *nirvana with remainder*, a synonym for residual cessation, which we discussed above. According to the lower schools, while the practitioner is in such a state, he or she makes a decision to either continue on the path or to remain in that place, accepting it as the final goal. If a practitioner makes the latter decision, upon passing away, his or her continuum ceases to exist, completely and forever.

In the sutras, an arhat, after death, is often compared to the image of a fire gone out after the supply of wood has been used up, or the flame of the lamp that is extinguished when the wick and oil run out. This kind of analogy indicates that everything is gone, that nothing exists after that state. Quoting such passages, the two lower schools maintain that certain beings by their own choice will not attain full enlightenment. For these schools, when parinirvana is achieved, not only does the form aggregate cease, but the mental aggregates do as well. Therefore, for these schools everything ceases, and there is no discussion of the continuation of consciousness. To me this seems to indicate that the delusions are completely integrated with the mind. As long as mind is there, delusions are there, and conversely when delusions cease the mind also ceases. Mahayana Buddhists believe that obscurations are not one with the mind, they are not completely integrated with the mind. They are temporary, or, to be more precise, adventitious. The basic nature of the mind is pure.

When the two higher schools talk about true cessation, therefore, they are not referring to the end of the practitioner's continuum but to the end of his or her karma and delusions. What continue are the truth body (Skt: *dharmakaya*), which is the enlightened aspect of the mental aggregates, and the form body (Skt: *rupakaya*), which is the enlightened aspect of the form aggregate.

A Buddha's Two Bodies

According to the Mahayana tradition, after achieving complete cessation, a practitioner not only realizes nirvana, but after death his or her now-purified form becomes the form body and his or her now-purified mental aggregates become the truth body.

The delusions cease but the mental continuum carries on, now completely purified and one with the compassion and wisdom that the practitioner has been developing since the start of the spiritual path. The mind that realizes emptiness directly and is full of compassion—in other words the mind of bodhichitta—is the base that becomes the truth body of a buddha.

The truth body has two different aspects: the mind realizing emptiness and the actual emptiness of that mind, so you often see literature that classifies the *dharmakaya* into two types: the wisdom truth body (Skt: *jnanakaya*), which is the mind of a buddha, and the natural truth body (Skt: *svabhavakaya*), which is the emptiness of the mind of a buddha.

In the same way, the form aggregate becomes the form body of a buddha. The gross physical body does not transmute into a buddha's gross physical body, as in some strange alchemical process. Rather the practitioner's gross physical aggregates dissolve, and the very subtle physical body becomes the base for the form body of the buddha he or she will become.

The form body is rarely talked about in Theravada. I see the concept of the form body as one of the big differences between the two traditions. *Rupakaya* does not necessarily mean material form. It really refers to how a buddha's omniscient mind of wisdom and compassion manifests in different forms. Since the only reason a buddha manifests is to aid other beings, and since there are different levels of beings with different levels of understanding, so there are different levels of that manifestation. These are commonly classified into two kinds: the enjoyment body (Skt: *sambhogakaya*) and the emanation body (Skt: *nirmanakaya*).

Some beings can see higher forms of a buddha's body, such as the complete enjoyment body. They can communicate with and receive teachings from the buddha in that form. Those who are realized enough to receive such teachings are arya beings and are already on the path of seeing. We will examine the five paths later. You often see Tibetan *tangka* paintings of buddhas in the *sambhogakaya* aspect, with beautiful robes and fine jewelry, as opposed to Shakyamuni Buddha's normal representation as a monk in simple monk's robes, which is his *nirmanakaya* aspect. From a Mahayana point of view, the historical Buddha, Shakyamuni, was a supreme emanation or *nirmanakaya*, because ordinary sentient beings were able to see him and receive teachings from him.

Buddhas can continuously and simultaneously emanate in many different forms and in many different places. When they began the path to enlightenment, their main aim was to benefit others, so of course when they achieve the result they must do that, otherwise they would be cheating! Therefore, the Mahayana tradition posits that when an individual achieves enlightenment, the two bodies—the truth and form bodies—manifest simultaneously. The truth body is the state of being free from obscurations; the form body is the form in which that being is perceived by others.

This is precisely why the Mahayana tradition emphasizes practicing both method and wisdom together—the method side produces the form body and the wisdom side produces the truth body. Bodhichitta, generosity, morality, and patience are all part of the method aspect of the path, which leads to the development of the form body of a buddha. Trying to achieve the wisdom that realizes emptiness and impermanence is the wisdom aspect, which leads to the development of the truth body.

If the form body of a buddha is a being, it is therefore impermanent, and so it might be argued that it is by nature suffering. Here again is a difference between the Theravada and Mahayana, this time in the interpretations of the four seals, Buddhism's fundamental tenets. The four seals are:

1. All compositional phenomena are impermanent.
2. All contaminated phenomena are, by nature, suffering.
3. All phenomena are empty of self-existence.
4. Nirvana is true peace.

Theravada scholars suggest that if something is impermanent it is contaminated, and therefore it is suffering. But Mahayana scholars, quoting the four seals, posit that while contaminated things are suffering, not all impermanent things are contaminated. They make a distinction. Things and events produced by afflictive emotions and karma are suffering because they are contaminated, but other impermanent things, such as a buddha's form body, are not necessarily suffering.

THE CONNECTION BETWEEN LIBERATION AND EMPTINESS

A famous quotation of Chandrakirti says:

Whether the Buddha comes into this world or not, emptinesses already exist.

It makes no difference whether a buddha comes into this world and teaches us about emptiness; all things and events, including our own existence, are still empty of inherent existence. However, it does take someone like Shakyamuni Buddha to have the wisdom to understand it and explain it to people like us in such a way that we can learn from it and actually come to realize it ourselves.

There is no difference between the fundamental nature of a table and the fundamental nature of my mind. Both are empty of inherent or intrinsic existence. Both require exactly the same process to realize, because both emptinesses are essentially identical. However, although objectively there is absolutely no difference between them, subjectively there is a big difference. My mind has all the adventitious delusions, such as anger, jealousy, fear—all the things caused by self-centeredness and self-cherishing—whereas a table has none of these. As long as my mind is obscured by all these delusions, it is very difficult to penetrate that fundamental nature, that absence of inherent existence. That makes the difference—but it does not mean that it is impossible.

There is a strong connection between liberation and emptiness. To understand liberation, we have to understand emptiness, otherwise we cannot see where we are caught up. The meaning of liberation is to be free from something. But it will never be more than the most abstract concept until we know what we need to be free from, and it is in the teachings on emptiness that we come to understand exactly what binds us. Fully realizing the nature of reality is the second of the obscurations, not the obscurations of defilements but the obscurations of knowledge.

The Four Characteristics of True Cessation

Like the other noble truths, the noble truth of the cessation of suffering has four unique characteristics. They are:

+ cessation
+ pacification
+ being superb
+ definite emergence

Like the other characteristics, these are specific qualities that belong uniquely to this noble truth and can help us fully understand and, in this case, realize it. The first quality, *cessation*, describes the noble truth itself—it is the ceasing of all delusions and ignorance, not only temporarily but forever. These negativities will never again occur in the mindstream.

The second characteristic is *pacification*. Cessation pacifies the torment of suffering, bringing the result of nirvana or enlightenment, complete and never-ending peace.

Because cessation is the ultimate goal of all spiritual paths, it is considered to be *superb*, the third characteristic, in the sense of being supreme in bringing about the source of all health and happiness. It is the quality of real trustworthiness, never changing or turning into something different or less supreme.

The fourth characteristic of cessation is that it will definitely bring us out of samsara, and so this characteristic is called *definite emergence*. By realizing the truth of the cessation of suffering, we are totally released from samsara and free from all sufferings and delusions.

5 THE TRUTH OF THE PATH

The Noble Eightfold Path and the Three Trainings

THE THREE PHASES

"Now this, bhikkhus, is the noble truth of the way leading to the cessation of suffering: it is this noble eightfold path; that is, right view, right intention, right speech, right action, right livelihood, right effort, right mindfulness, right concentration....

"'This noble truth of the way leading to the cessation of suffering is to be developed': thus, bhikkhus, in regard to things unheard before, there arose in me vision, knowledge, wisdom, true knowledge, and light.

"'This noble truth of the way leading to the cessation of suffering has been developed': thus, bhikkhus, in regard to things unheard before, there arose in me vision, knowledge, wisdom, true knowledge, and light."

IN THIS VERSION OF THE SUTRA, which, again, is a translation of the Pali, the first phase of the nature of the truth of the path leading to cessation is described as the noble eightfold path. This differs from the Tibetan translation of the Sanskrit version, which makes no specific mention of the noble eightfold path. Although this path is not often emphasized in Tibetan Buddhism, it is implicitly taught as part of the thirty-seven paths to enlightenment, and as one of the groups of paths that lead to cessation.

In the second phase the Buddha explains what the practitioner should do with regard to this truth—cultivate or develop it—and in the third phase, the Buddha explains the ultimate result, or complete attainment. Once the practitioner fully cultivates the paths, such as the noble eightfold path or the five paths, he or she reaches the final attainment. This cultivation never deteriorates.

The Path to Enlightenment

The last noble truth, the path leading to the cessation of suffering, actually encompasses the entire spiritual journey that we need to undertake if we are ever to be free of suffering. Every positive action we have ever done is related to this last noble truth in some way. It is a long path, and we must not become discouraged. In that regard I find the words of His Holiness the Dalai Lama very inspiring:

> Another important factor is your determination. You should not imagine that all these developments can take place within a few days or a few years; they may even take several aeons, so determination is evidently vital. If you consider yourself a Buddhist and want to really practice Buddha Dharma, then right from the start you must make up your mind to do so until the end, regardless of whether it takes millions or billions of aeons.
>
> After all, what is the meaning of our life? In itself, there is no intrinsic meaning. However if we use life in a positive way, then even the days and the months and the aeons can become meaningful. On the other hand, if you just fritter your life away

aimlessly then even one day feels too long. You will find that once you have a firm determination and a clear objective, then time is not important.

As Shantideva writes in this beautiful prayer:

As long as space endures
As long as sentient beings remain,
Until then may I too remain
To dispel the miseries of the world.[23]

These inspiring words say so much to me. The more impatient we are, and the more we want to find the way that is easiest or cheapest, the more likely we are to obtain a poor result. So I suggest this is the wrong approach.

In searching for a path that leads to liberation and enlightenment, we look for a way to deal with the afflictive emotions that have been with us since we first started to interact with other beings. To confront such deep-rooted emotions, determination is not enough—we must also develop a clear objective, a clear idea of what we are looking for. Without that, our determination will definitely be unstable.

Our objective must be to search for the true, complete cessation of our afflictive emotions—not just some, not just at a certain level, but long-term and complete. We must aim for true cessation, which is the complete destruction of our fears and anxieties. The path we settle upon must have the power to bring this about. Of course, before we reach complete cessation, we need immediate solutions to sort out our daily difficulties, but our ultimate aim must always go beyond that. It must address the very root of our problems.

Whereas both the Theravada and Mahayana traditions agree that the essence of the path that leads to cessation was taught by the Buddha as the noble eightfold path, in the Mahayana tradition there is a sense that the eight aspects of this path are tools that lead us to a direct, intuitive understanding of emptiness—the ultimate path to buddhahood. In Theravada, the noble eightfold path is seen as an end in itself, incorporating the understanding of emptiness within it. Rahula says that each of the 84,000 discourses of the Buddha can be classified within one of the eight categories of the eightfold noble path.[24] His Holiness the Dalai Lama says that the true path should be understood in terms of developing a direct intuitive realization of emptiness.[25] This is what really leads to the complete cessation of all afflictive emotions. Although there is absolutely no contradiction between these two statements, the emphasis is different, and for this reason in Mahayana we focus more on the study and practice of the three trainings and the five paths and less on the noble eightfold path.

THE MANY PATHS IN BUDDHISM

It might seem strange that you can study Buddhism within one tradition and never hear the term *noble eightfold path* or study it within another tradition and never hear the term *five paths*. This situation stems from the different approaches each system uses rather than some inherent contradiction. Buddhism developed from a monastic and decidedly oral tradition, and thus many of the teachings we have today come from textbooks for monks or nuns. This is especially true in Tibet, where days in the monastery seem to be full of memorizing lists!

In one of the sutras, the Buddha describes the thirty-seven aspects of enlightenment, from which many of our lists have derived. The thirty-seven aspects are: the four mindfulnesses, the four complete abandonments, the four factors of miraculous powers, the five faculties, the five powers, the seven branches of the path to enlightenment, and the noble eightfold path.

The first of these, the four mindfulnesses, is very much emphasized within the Theravada teachings but is hardly ever discussed within the Mahayana. This does not mean that Mahayanists are not mindful but rather that these teachings are subsumed into other lists—in this case they are incorporated into the five paths. In fact, in the Mahayana tradition the noble eightfold path is also subsumed within the five paths. Both the four mindfulnesses and the noble eightfold path are discrete practices that are developed from the beginning to the advanced stages, whereas the five paths reflect the degree of attainment of all the practices. They are different paradigms rather than competing systems. The thirty-seven aspects of enlightenment are explicit within the Theravada teachings, but are incorporated within the Mahayana teachings on the five paths.

THE THREE TRAININGS

Important to both Mahayana and Theravada are the three trainings. They are:

- ✦ ethics (Skt: *shila*)
- ✦ concentration (Skt: *samadhi*)
- ✦ wisdom (Skt: *prajna*)

Within these three divisions we can include the entire noble eightfold path:

right speech
right action   } ethics
right livelihood

right effort
right mindfulness   } concentration
right concentration

right view
right thought $\Big\}$ wisdom

The first training, ethics (also called ethical conduct or moral discipline) is crucial in developing the second and the third, concentration and wisdom, and as such is really the foundation for the other two.

What is morally right and wrong is something that each of us feels intuitively, even when it is not taught to us by our parents or our teachers. Ethics must be based on compassion, not on some commitment that we follow simply because we are Buddhists and have been told to practice it. By understanding compassion, we see how ethical conduct is required, and as we develop compassion, ethical behavior will arise quite spontaneously.

Nothing is intrinsically immoral from its own side. "Moral" or "immoral" can be defined by the way an individual person communicates with others, or how they mentally perceive others. So ethical conduct, practicing a moral life, is not something that can effectively be enforced from the outside but must grow out of a subjective understanding of what helps and what harms others. Therefore, whether something is moral or not really depends on whether others' feelings and rights have been considered. That is where compassion comes in. If we live our lives taking into account others' feelings, perspectives, and rights, then basically we are living an ethical life.

At the initial stage, particularly within modern Western society, ethics is the most relevant of the three trainings. Ethics is where we most often fall short in our everyday lives. This is not to say that the other two trainings are not important or relevant at our present stage of development. Ethics flounders without mindfulness and the sense of the interconnectedness of all beings that studying emptiness brings.

But for most lay people leading a normal working life, I feel that the emphasis should be on ethical conduct, because every day we have to deal with others and make moral choices.

Although as Buddhists our main objective is to achieve true, complete cessation, in order to reach it we have to overcome more immediate problems. Dealing with jobs, the society we live in, trying to give our children the best, and so forth can lead to a narrowing of our outlook and an emphasis on our own or our family's happiness above the happiness of others. This applies to the Sangha as well, of course, and monks and nuns are as capable as lay people of being unethical, but within a monastic environment they are less at risk.

Ethical conduct is basic. I'm not talking about commitments given by a teacher, such as the *pratimoksha* vows, but something more general. Buddhist practitioners might worry about the meaning of some vows they have taken, but everyone agrees that cheating somebody, whether you believe in a religion or not, is unethical.

Buddhism goes deeper than conventional thinking in its exhortations to us to avoid unethical actions. We avoid harming others not simply because the actions themselves might have obviously negative repercussions, but because the mind that generates an unethical action will cause suffering for ourselves and others in less discernable ways in the future. As with everything in Buddhism, the motivation is crucial. A fully ordained monk has a vow to avoid beating somebody with a straw. Although the action causes no physical harm, if the motivation is to harm somebody, it has harmful repercussions. Avoiding that sort of harmful motivation is part of training in ethics.

The second training, which includes concentration and mindfulness, leads to the ability to focus our minds on whatever object we choose, and to keep that focus clearly and with intensity for an extended period of time. Concentration in itself is neutral. Whether it is positive or negative depends on the object of our concentration.

Living an immoral life tends to mean focusing on sense pleasures and indulgences at the expense of others and often that means a very dissipated life. Therefore, immorality and concentration rarely go together. So in order to have a single-pointed mind, living an ethical life is essential. On the basis of an ethical life, we can slowly develop our concentration from the very simple mindfulness meditations emphasized in Theravada, such as observing the body posture or the breath, to practices that develop more clarity and extended concentration. When we are really advanced we can actually develop true calm abiding.

Wisdom, the understanding of how things and events really exist in terms of their impermanence, interdependence, and lack of intrinsic existence, is the third training, and again its foundation is the other two trainings, especially concentration. Even an intellectual understanding of wisdom requires focus, and this is even more true if we wish to take this understanding to a depth where it really starts to turn our life around.

As with the other two trainings, training in wisdom progresses through levels. Our practice grows gradually from a study of the mind, specifically the wrong concepts we labor under, and develops through the different subtleties of the law of cause and effect until we can come to understand and eventually realize emptiness and impermanence.

All three trainings are deeply interlinked. In order to have wisdom, we must have concentration; in order to have concentration, we need ethics. But developing ethics requires a degree of wisdom and concentration as well. Although we do not have to perfect the first training before we can start on the second, and in fact it is imperative that they develop together, there is still a sequence in terms of the emphasis we place on each.

The *dharmachakra*, the Dharma wheel,[26] symbolizes these three trainings, with the center ring at the hub representing ethical conduct. This

The Dharma Wheel

shows that ethics is the foundation of everything. The eight spokes represent wisdom, their spikes protruding from the rim—like Manjushri's sword—cutting through ignorance, and the external rim represents the concentration that supports wisdom.

At present we probably avoid lying and stealing because of the fear of punishment. Although the motivation may be the fear of the results of karma rather than the reprimand of a teacher or parent, this is still a quite childish perspective. When we finally develop a right view about how things exist and how we are all interdependent, our minds naturally become ethical. However, this is probably a long way off, and we need ethical behavior now. Seeing that practicing ethics does bring positive results right now spurs us into continuing and expanding our practice.

I sometimes feel for the smokers who take the eight Mahayana precepts during our retreats. It must be really challenging. If they see the positive results and not just the agony of nicotine withdrawal, however, it might encourage them to take things further. The technique is to start with an ethical base you are comfortable with and slowly build on it.

Ethics

If you read treatises such as Maitreya's *Ornament of Clear Realization* (*Abhisamayalamkara*), you will find the noble eightfold path explained in the context of a bodhisattva who has realized emptiness directly and is on the path of seeing. For us, I feel it is more useful to simply describe each category of the noble eightfold path very loosely in terms of how we ordinary people might actually practice it here and now.

The first three of the noble eightfold path—right speech, right action, and right livelihood—are part of the first training, ethics. Living ethically by practicing these three definitely gives us the foundation to do the other practices, whereas living without them, in an undisciplined way, causes all sorts of obstacles to developing concentration or wisdom. If we do not live our lives with right speech, right action, and right livelihood, it is very difficult to find the techniques we need in order to develop a path that leads us to cessation. Even if we practice the most sophisticated method of visualization or meditation within highest yoga tantra, we will not succeed.

Speech is one of our main instruments of communication, and right speech means understanding the consequences of what we say and how we say it. Because we constantly use speech to convey what we think to others, being mindful that our speech does not harm them is a very important practice. This of course relates back to the four actions of speech from the ten nonvirtues—lying, divisive speech, harsh words, and gossip—that we already discussed. There are also four related virtues—the direct opposites of their nonvirtues—that should be cultivated to enhance this practice of right speech. They are:

speaking the truth	lying
bringing foes together	divisive speech
speaking peacefully and politely	harsh words
speaking meaningfully	idle gossip

Right speech consists of both being mindful of avoiding the non-virtues of speech and deliberately cultivating the opposing virtuous actions. It is all about not harming others and, instead, helping them.

Similarly, the practice of right action can be seen as abandoning the three nonvirtues of body and cultivating the corresponding three virtuous actions. They are:

protecting the lives of others	killing
practicing great generosity	stealing
maintaining moral conduct	sexual misconduct

Protecting the lives of others includes everything from the heroic act of saving someone from a burning building to taking an insect out of the bath before we shower. It can also be active restraint from killing, such as when we overcome the desire to spray the flowers in our garden with insecticide. Generosity and ethics are two of the six perfections, and we can practice these things in many small ways every day, gradually increasing the extent of our practice and integrating it with our consciousness.

The remaining virtuous actions correspond to the three nonvirtues of the mind. The section on wisdom below covers the substance of these, so we will not discuss them here.

non-attachment	covetousness
loving-kindness	harmful intent
right view	wrong views

Right livelihood is very important. To live, most of us have to earn a wage, particularly in this very competitive world. However, and perhaps it is a mark of how aggressive Western society is, if we look closely, very few jobs do not actively harm others. I therefore feel this concept of right livelihood requires serious consideration. As far as we can, we need to live a life that avoids consciously harming others and consequently the way we earn our living should be as pure as possible.

Of course, in some situations this might be impossible. With even a simple job, it can be very difficult to measure the effects we have on others, and even when we try to avoid harming others, it can still happen. Sometimes, also, it is unavoidable. I recently talked to a woman who had been unemployed for two years and had applied for a job. She is a very honest person. The job was very important to her, and she could see it could be of great benefit, but if she answered the questions scrupulously honestly on the application, she knew she would not get the job. In an era where the "creative C. V." is almost a positive thing, she was really worried about the need to lie and asked my advice, but I didn't know how to help her. Things are rarely black and white. She needed to look at what would be most beneficial overall. So on the one hand maybe she needed to answer those questions in whatever way necessary to get the job, but on the other hand, being strictly honest might be better in the long run.

Right livelihood does not necessarily mean that everything we do to earn a living must be precise and scrupulously honest no matter what. Inevitably difficult decisions will arise. But if we consciously pay attention to how we are living and what we need to do to develop spiritually, then whatever we do will be right livelihood.

Of course if you are reading this book, you are not likely to trade arms with terrorists or actively poison water sources. But look at the company you work for and see what effect they are having on the environment and the people in that environment; see what damage is being done. Even if we personally are not doing anything wrong, if our livelihood is based on something even slightly harmful, subconsciously something happens. That mental state will always disturb our mind.

Right livelihood goes beyond the job we do, to the effect we have

on the environment and even what we eat. For example, eating vegetables seems less harmful than eating meat, but farmers use chemicals
when they grow vegetables, and many beings, such as insects and birds,
are killed. If we can avoid harming others, we should, but we should
at least do as little harm as possible. Being mindful of such things is
an important part of our practice.

It seems no matter what we do we are still complicit in harming others by what we consume. Of course, it is good to be mindful, but it is
also good to be realistic. We are citizens of a world where big business
has control, and I think only a fanatic could live without compromise
in any way. The goal is spiritual development, and fanaticism will not
get us there. We have to live and we need material things to survive,
and as far as possible we should get them without causing harm to others.

These three—right speech, right action, and right livelihood—really
help to lay down the foundation for our journey to liberation because
they are concerned with the ethics aspect of the three trainings.

Concentration

Right effort, right mindfulness, and right concentration, as listed in
the noble eightfold path, are connected with concentration or mental
discipline. Living a moral life based on these three is a key factor in
developing concentration. Right mindfulness, the mind that can hold
an object, is especially vital.

For beginners like us, learning a simple meditation technique and
keeping it going is very difficult because we are so easily distracted.
We need to develop stable mindfulness in order to maintain our awareness on the object of meditation. Right effort can be used in many
ways, but with mindfulness, we can see how right effort is crucial in
overcoming the force of our habitual tendencies. Our mind is scattered
all the time, even during sleep, and without right effort, our mindfulness will never be strong.

Sometimes this practice is also called *joyous effort*. It takes genuine, sincere joy from our hearts to accomplish anything positive. In this case, really understanding the motivation and the result is vital. Without a clear understanding of the intentions behind our actions, our motivation will be weak and our determination to develop will falter. Right effort—doing something positive with a clear, strong motivation—helps us to refrain from negative actions as well as make our nonharming attitude more grounded and solid. In that way, although right effort can be subsumed into the training of concentration, it is applicable to all practices.

The second practice is right mindfulness. Mindfulness is heavily emphasized in the Theravada tradition, and I feel that it is both very powerful and very much needed in our daily lives. In fact, to practice right speech, right action, and right livelihood, we need right mindfulness. Without it, we will make so many mistakes. Mindfulness on a practical level is merely being aware of what is going on around us. In the context of meditation and concentration, it means the ability of the mind to stay on the object of concentration. I am not really sure how far this practice alone can take us toward the main goal of achieving complete cessation, or how effective it is in dealing with our afflictive emotions. Having said that, right mindfulness is crucial because we need it to see what is going on in our minds.

Many methods exist for developing basic mindfulness. At the initial stage, we learn how to bring our scattered minds to focus on the sensations within our bodies in the present moment. It is a very simple technique. We then learn how to prolong that awareness, and on that basis we subsequently develop some clarity, where the mind is less obscured, less fuzzy. We can do this by simply observing our body posture, not giving it any labels—right, wrong, pain, pleasure— just being with our bodies. We can also concentrate on the breath, counting our inhalations and exhalations as we focus on either the sensation of the air at our nostrils or the movement of our abdomen.

Of course, just because mindfulness is simple does not mean that it is easy. It can be a lifetime's practice. Mindfulness has three distinct aspects: stability, clarity, and intensity. Although we can work on all three together, we really need to master one before we can get very far with the next. At first we try to develop a stable mind for a longer and longer duration, not worrying too much about how clearly the object is appearing to the mind. But once we can hold the object for a long time, our focus switches to the clarity aspect. As we develop this, we begin to see that our awareness might be clear, but it has varying degrees of intensity—it may have clarity but be quite weak. And so we then start to cultivate the intensity of the awareness. This is not something you master in a weekend course!

Right concentration refers to the single-pointed mind. With mindfulness holding the object, the mind focuses on that object. If it is an object like compassion, the single-pointed mind actually *becomes* compassion. This is one difference between mindfulness and concentration. Although both minds share qualities, mindfulness is merely the ability to hold an object; it can never become the object. With mindfulness, whatever we do will be very effective. Concentration is crucial for meditations on selflessness and the like—without it even a meditation on compassion will be very scattered, and it will take a long time to develop any result. Single-pointed concentration is a very powerful tool, and there are many different techniques for developing it. To go into detail would require a whole book.

Wisdom

The last two of the noble eightfold path, right view and right thought, refer to developing wisdom and pure motivation. Right view can also be called *right understanding*.

Right view can be put into three levels. A very basic right view is simply common sense, seeing things that are wise or beneficial to do, such as believing in the law of causality. Even without a precise understanding, it still benefits us to have some sort of conviction in the Buddha and in the other great masters who have taught that following the law of causality is the right thing to do.

At this stage we hold a very elementary notion of what samsara is—we know that we are in samsara due to delusions and karma and that if we do not deal with them we will be in this condition forever. Even though we may not have a precise understanding and simply trust the great masters, this trust evokes a very basic right view. This can subsequently progress into actual understanding, as when we take our study of the four noble truths to the point where we are firmly convinced of the law of causality. Holding this kind of view can be called right view, as can an understanding of the more gross levels of selflessness, such as feeling that there is no person separate from our aggregates or that all contaminated things bring suffering. This is an intermediate right view. The goal is to understand emptiness intuitively, beyond the intellectual, but we need words and concepts to get there. The process moves from the rational to the intuitive.

The most refined right view is the view that all things and events are empty of intrinsic existence, that not a single phenomenon exists that does not depend on others. *Others* here means other phenomena, not necessarily beings; it could even be a concept or a name.

Right thought refers mainly to correct intention or motivation. Say, for instance, a person has gained a direct realization of emptiness. This person can explain emptiness to others, but if any self-interest is present at all, it cannot be called right thought. The motivation must be purely to benefit others, without any conscious or subconscious thought of payback in any form. Similarly, if someone practices generosity by giving away their possessions, if they have any sense of wanting something in return, it is also not right thought.

When trying to practice Dharma, our motivation must be, at the very least, a sincere wish to confront our own delusions and negative karma. This kind of thought is right thought. If any other motivation clouds our practice, such as the wish for recognition, power, or wealth, then no matter how strong our Dharma practice might be, it is not right thought because the intention is not pure.

The practices of generosity, morality, patience, joyous effort, concentration, and wisdom are wonderful and very positive things, but without right thought they cannot be called the practice of the six perfections. Each must be fueled by pure motivation, untouched by any self-interest. Right thought is practicing Dharma with pure motivation, conscientiously trying to eliminate all delusions and negative karma from our mindstreams, especially to gain enlightenment in order to be of most benefit to others.

Nihilism and eternalism

From the Mahayana Buddhist perspective, right view is the understanding of emptiness, the highest wisdom that sees ultimate reality. This realization is also called right view because it is free from the two extremes, nihilism and eternalism.

A totally correct view of reality requires a lot of rational discrimination, otherwise we easily fall into one or the other extreme. We are generally trapped in the view of the world as concrete and distinct from the mind that observes it. This innacurate view is dangerous because it creates a sense of alienation that causes us to engage in harmful acts. So it is necessary to understand how this is not so, and how what we see as real and concrete is really much like an illusion.

The first extreme is nihilism, the view that nothing exists. There is a huge difference between seeing life as *like* an illusion, as Mahayana

Buddhism proposes, and actually thinking that life *is* an illusion. To believe that nothing actually exists destroys all conviction about cause and effect and therefore all motivation to avoid nonvirtue and develop virtue. Everything, in short, becomes meaningless, all actions pointless.

Nihilism is more dangerous than skepticism or eternalism because it is a very subtle perversion of the inquiry the mind needs to make in order to understand reality. Breaking down the conception of concrete reality that dogs us at present, we need to develop ever subtler views. There is a very fine line between the most subtle view and the view in which all reality simply vanishes. The deconstruction of the way we perceive things has gone too far if we no longer find anything that exists. This nihilistic view can be argued very persuasively by well-educated and well-meaning people.

The other extreme is eternalism, the view that something is eternally unchangeable without depending on other things. It is generally not an intellectual construct at all but something we all instinctively hold onto.

Between these two extremes are many levels, and treading the middle way that keeps us from falling into either extreme can seem like walking a tightrope, requiring as it does such subtle discriminations. For this reason right view cannot be reached purely by right thought, by good intention. We need a lot of rational inquiry as well.

But as with everything to do with the spiritual path, if our examination remains on the intellectual level, it is utterly useless. We need to take our understanding of right view to a level in which it becomes part of our natural outlook and informs our relationship with the external world. The traditional analogy is seeing white snow-covered mountains as yellow because of jaundice, although I suppose today we could change this to wearing sunglasses. Rationally, we know the mountains are white, but we see them as yellow. If we relate to them as if they are yellow, even though logically we know this is not so, it is incorrect. We need to "take off the sunglasses" and see the snow-covered mountains as they really are. Therefore, the process of developing right view, of actually seeing everything as it is, is very difficult and takes a long time.

Being on the Path

THE FIVE PATHS

If you ask a Theravada master to teach the last noble truth, he or she will explain the noble eightfold path. If you ask a Tibetan master, he or she will present the five paths. The five paths are:

1. the path of accumulation
2. the path of preparation
3. the path of seeing
4. the path of meditation
5. the path of no more learning

These five paths might seem completely unrelated to the noble eightfold path, but in fact they are just a different paradigm for the same spiritual journey. The noble eightfold path describes the different aspects of the journey, such as ethics and concentration, and the five paths describe the different levels attained on that journey. Simply put, the noble eightfold path is like the subjects you can study at a university, whereas the five paths are like the levels of that study—bachelor, masters, and doctorate.

Many people have asked me why Tibetan Buddhism does not present the noble eightfold path as part of the fourth noble truth, but for me there is no difference between the noble eightfold path and the five paths apart from the style of presentation. In the Mahayana tradition, when the path leading to cessation is presented in the context of the five paths, the noble eightfold path is implicit. The noble eightfold path is the substance, and the five paths is the process, the step-by-step progress that we have to make.

The path of accumulation

The first path is called the *path of accumulation* because on this path we have not yet reached the level on which we can integrate our practice fully into our mindstreams, but are still accumulating the right material, information, and merit to get us there. *Accumulation* refers to more than intellectual acquisition and includes the development of mental qualities such as mindfulness. Understanding what positive things we need to accumulate and what negative things we need to avoid, of course, leads us back to the noble eightfold path.

We need to collect the very basic necessities for our journey to liberation and enlightenment, such as the determination to be free from samsara (renunciation) and the understanding of impermanence. It is easy to see that here *accumulation* refers to a stage in the development of these properties rather than some dry accumulation of knowledge. The practices remain at the path of accumulation because there is still no real *direct* realization of whatever aspect of the eightfold path we are considering. That is not to say that our meditation practice is not advanced, but that we have yet to go beyond the conceptual understanding of the subjects we are meditating on. At this level we are accumulating those skills, as well as accumulating the positive mental energy—the merit—we need to get further.

The path of preparation

When we have enough information and have developed our skills sufficiently, we slowly pass beyond a conceptual understanding of the subject and begin to have moments where the meditation on something like emptiness becomes more intuitive. When this happens, we reach the path of preparation.

At this point we already have a very deep conceptual understanding of impermanence or emptiness and have achieved the very advanced state of single-pointed meditation called calm abiding. By combining the two and testing this conceptual understanding again and again, we achieve what is known as the *union of calm abiding and special insight,* and we will be able to break through into an intuitive understanding of the subject. We will be able to *perceive* emptiness or impermanence rather than just *conceive* of it.

Preparation here refers to preparing the way for the eventual direct realization of emptiness or impermanence. It is the final breaking down, through the union of calm abiding and special insight, of the subtle, intellectually held wrong views that block our direct perception. We are not quite there, though, at this point, as some very subtle obscurations are still coming between the subject—the mind—and the object of meditation—emptiness.

The path of seeing

When we do finally break through and perceive emptiness directly, we achieve the next path, the path of seeing. Moving beyond conceptual understanding, we can now *see* emptiness directly. At this level we are called *arya* beings because of this remarkable attribute. For the first time in our countless lifetimes we see reality as it actually is. This is where the *noble* of four noble truths comes from—they are truths to an arya being.

On the path of seeing, this direct realization of emptiness is the real antidote to eliminating not only our intellectually held wrong views, but also their seeds. Within our meditation sessions we realize emptiness directly with increasing facility, although outside the meditation session we revert to the perceptions of the conceptual mind, albeit a very refined conceptuality.

As this stage continues, the mind becomes subtler and stronger, and we abandon both the intellectually acquired wrong views as well as the innate wrong views, including their seeds.

The path of meditation

At this stage we no longer have gross self-grasping or any wrong view, but imprints of the most subtle innate obscurations remain. In order to eliminate them we need to move beyond intermittent direct realizations of emptiness to the stage in which we are in constant meditation with a continuous direct realization.

This is the path of meditation, although the "meditation" referred to here is something much more advanced than what we normally picture when we hear this word. Within the Tibetan Buddhist tradition, the word *meditation* (Tib: *gom*) refers to habituating the mind to an object—inferring a positive one such as compassion or the visualization of a buddha. Having gone beyond conceptual understanding and even beyond intermittent direct realization, a constant state of direct perception of reality is needed to finally wear away the most subtle innate obscurations that keep us from enlightenment.

The path of no more learning

When the last, most subtle obscurations finally cease, we achieve complete cessation or enlightenment. At this point there is nothing more to do, nothing more to learn—hence it is called the *path of no more learning*. *No more learning* and *enlightenment* are in fact synonyms, the former describing the stage we reach and the latter describing the state we attain.

You have probably noticed that everything I am speaking of relates to emptiness or impermanence, the wisdom side of the path, and that the five paths depict a clear and natural progression from the intellectual and conceptual to the intuitive and perceptual. However, a point of great discussion in the debating yards of the Tibetan monasteries is how the method aspect of the path fits into all of this. At what stage does the emotional component of the practice become direct? Many great masters believe that although we need bodhichitta to attain the path of accumulation, it will never become a direct realization until we reach this very last stage of no more learning.

THE INDIVIDUAL LIBERATION PRACTITIONER AND THE BODHISATTVAYANA PRACTITIONER

As I mentioned above, there is a basic difference of approach between the practitioner following the path of individual liberation and the Mahayana practitioner following the path leading to enlightenment using what can be called the *Bodhisattvayana*. Both practitioners must progress through the same process of the five paths of accumulation, preparation, seeing, meditation, and no more learning. In relation to the final path, however, there is a big difference. On the individual path, the term *no more learning* represents the fact that the practitioner has attained freedom from samsara. When the practitioner reaches that state, there is no more learning.

In fact, the main difference between the two vehicles on this point comes not from the wisdom side of the practice, as both define this path by the consistent presence of a direct realization of emptiness, but from the method side. The individual vehicle practitioner does not need bodhichitta, so according to the scriptures of this vehicle, the stage of no more learning can be achieved in a few lifetimes. The core of the Bodhisattvayana practitioner's practice, however, is to develop bodhichitta, and this can take eons. This shows how much more difficult the bodhisattva's goal is—to achieve a mind that sees no difference between self and others and that cherishes oneself and all others equally. Compared to that, realizing selflessness is easy!

This is a tricky point and can easily be misconstrued. It is easy to conclude that Mahayana scholars believe that practitioners on the path of individual liberation do things out of self-interest and are hence "selfish," but in fact that is not so. To think that individual liberation practitioners can gain liberation, which requires a realization of selflessness, but can still be self-centered is totally illogical. However, although a practitioner of the individual vehicle does in fact have to confront the *self-grasping* mind—the mind that grasps on to a concept of a "real" self—this practitioner does not necessarily have to confront the *self-cherishing* mind, the mind that sees oneself as more precious than others. Of course, it is impossible to think about the eightfold noble path, no matter how superficially, without realizing that the practitioner on the individual liberation path must consider others and work toward their welfare, but this practice does not emphasize taking responsibility for the ultimate well-being of all sentient beings. In fact, in order to make the most progress, a practitioner of the individual vehicle probably needs to withdraw from the world, and effectively push the welfare of others to one side.

If we accept that such practitioners do not need to deal with the self-cherishing mind, we must also realize that self-cherishing has many different levels. There is no way to compare the self-cherishing mind of the true practitioners on the path of individual liberation with the self-cherishing mind we presently have. Our self-cherishing mind is so gross; their self-cherishing by contrast is far subtler.

A person on the bodhisattva path is trying to overcome self-cherishing, but in fact, while on the path, a certain self-cherishing can be useful. Taking responsibility for others, if done skillfully, is a source of happiness both for the practitioner and the beings that he or she helps. So if the wish for personal happiness is mixed with that practitioner's motivation, then that type of self-cherishing does not bring problems. This is the skillful way to cherish ourselves, whereas the unskillful way is to cherish ourselves to the exclusion of others.

To reach the beginning of the path of accumulation, both types of practitioner need the spontaneous determination to be free from samsara. However, a Bodhisattvayana practitioner also needs the strong, spontaneous determination to achieve genuine bodhichitta, to attain full enlightenment for the sake of all sentient beings. Perhaps you took the bodhisattva vows when you received an initiation from a lama. The bodhichitta discussed in that situation is called *aspirational bodhichitta*. Here, bodhichitta refers to the actual mind that constantly and fully devotes itself to others.

WHEN ARE WE ACTUALLY ON THE PATH?

The great Tibetan master and founder of the Gelug tradition, Lama Tsongkhapa, states unequivocally that a person is on the path of accumulation of an individual practitioner only when they have developed the strong spontaneous determination to be free from samsara. Without that, no matter how much intellectual knowledge you have, or how great a meditator you are, you cannot even claim to be on the first path. For the practitioner on the Bodhisattvayana path, however, the demarcation is even greater; that practitioner needs the attainment of genuine bodhichitta to enter the path of accumulation.

Much of Buddhist teaching is about cutting desire, but it seems that we need an incredibly strong desire to be free of samsara to actually progress spiritually. Is there a contradiction here? We normally associate desire with craving sense pleasures such as chocolate or sex, but in fact desire can be positive or negative. Desiring to be free from samsara is a positive desire and one that will never cause problems. However, having a very strong desire for samsaric things, no matter what they are, sooner or later brings dissatisfaction.

It is impossible to have both desire for samsara and desire to be free from samsara at the same time. In Tibet we have this food called *tsampa,* which is ground barley flour. Breakfast for many Tibetans is still simply tea and tsampa, which is popped dry into the mouth. Trying to live with one foot in samsara and one foot in nirvana is compared to trying to play the flute while having your mouth full of tsampa. Utterly impossible! Ultimately we have to choose; we cannot have both. In the same way, a strong spontaneous determination to be free from samsara and attachment to samsaric things cannot arise simultaneously.

Attachment is the problem, not necessarily desire, and the two words are often confused. Attachment is always negative, whereas desire can be either. If we have the desire, the strong sincere determination, to attain buddhahood or liberation, there is no room for attachment. This aspiration is positive.

There are two basic ways to cultivate this determination. One way is to see the root of samsara, which means seeing emptiness and seeing the need to be free from the wrong view of self-grasping. The other way is to see the true disadvantages of being in samsara. Both methods are equally valid; either can be cultivated, and eventually they will come together. Each method is merely the starting point determined by the propensities of the practitioner.

The Four Characteristics of the Truth of the Path

As with the other noble truths, the truth of the path leading to the cessation of suffering has its four unique characteristics. They are:

+ path
+ awareness

✦ achievement
✦ deliverance

The first one, *path*, is the means by which we progress, such as the noble eightfold path or the five paths. These practices are "paths" that will lead to cessation in the same way that certain streets will lead to our desired destination.

The various paths also all have the second characteristic, *awareness*, which is the ability of these paths to lead us to a full and complete understanding of what the root of cyclic existence is, and thus lead us to escape it. We become aware of both the depth of our problems and the means of escape.

The third characteristic, *achievement*, is similar to the second characteristic. However, here it is presented from the perspective of the resultant state, which means that through these various paths we can *definitely* achieve the result of liberation or enlightenment. Awareness means to know what is right and what is wrong, whereas achievement means the actual practice that gets you there. They refer to aspects of the same thing. If someone says, "Geshe Tashi," or uses my other name, Lhundrub Pelba, they are referring to the same person but using different words. In the conceptual world, these names may create slightly different pictures—not pictures of different people but of different aspects of the same person. In the same way, awareness is what gets you there and achievement is what you get.

The fourth characteristic is called *deliverance* because it destroys the main cause of samsara. The noble eightfold path has the quality of deliverance, delivering us from the bondage of our conditioned existence.

THE SIXTEEN CHARACTERISTICS OF THE FOUR NOBLE TRUTHS

	1. impermanence
the first noble truth	2. suffering
the truth of suffering	3. emptiness
	4. selflessness
	5. causes
the second noble truth	6. origin
the truth of origin	7. strong production
	8. condition
	9. cessation
the third noble truth	10. pacification
the truth of cessation	11. being superb
	12. definite emergence
	13. path
the fourth noble truth	14. awareness
the truth of the path	15. achievement
	16. deliverance

In the Mahayana tradition we develop the realization of the four noble truths through the understanding of these sixteen characteristics. Furthermore, the characteristics can be developed though progression on each of the five paths, from the path of accumulation to the path of no more learning. During the path of accumulation they are understood at a very basic level, then understood more deeply at the stage of the path of preparation, and so on.

Studying the four noble truths and developing an understanding of them, really contemplating them and through that process developing a deep realization, is a crucial process for a Buddhist practitioner. This is the reason why the Buddha taught the four noble truths as his first teaching, the reason he taught it on many other occasions, and the reason it was his last teaching before passing into parinirvana.

Whatever we read on Buddhism, whatever teaching we hear or retreat we attend, no matter how simple and pragmatic or how esoteric, it can always be related back to one of the topics within the four noble truths. They are the font from which all the other teachings flow. They are the matrix upon which all the other teachings are set. Our goal is the attainment of wisdom and compassion, but we cannot even begin that journey without a clear understanding of our current situation. It is only from studying the four noble truths that that understanding will grow.

As a Buddhist practitioner, understanding the four noble truths is really the main education—if I can use that word—upon which to set up our entire Buddhist practice. In fact, the four noble truths encompass all Buddhist teaching.

NOTES

1   *Setting the Wheel of Dharma in Motion* (Pali: *Dammacakkappavattana-sutta*), translated by Bhikku Bodhi in *The Connected Discourses of the Buddha* (Boston: Wisdom Publications, 2000), 1843–46.

2   Holmes, Ken and Katia, *The Changeless Nature: A Translation of Maitreya's Uttaratantra* (UK: Karma Drubgyud Darjay Ling, 1985), 134.

3   Gyatso, Tenzin, the Fourteenth Dalai Lama, *The Four Noble Truths* (London: Thorsons, 1997), 34.

4   *The Dhammapada, The Path to Perfection.* Trans. Juan Mascaro, (UK: Penguin Books Ltd, 1973), V276. Mara denotes the delusions, often mythologized as a demon.

5   Carus, Paul, ed., "The Sermon at Benares," in *The Gospel of Buddha*, (1915; repr., UK: Alcove Press Ltd, 1974), 50–51. This passage appears to be a free paraphrase of the sutra rather than a perfect translation, although it is evocative nonetheless.

6   Gyatso, Tenzin, the Fourteenth Dalai Lama, *Ethics for the New Millennium*, (New York: Riverhead, 1999), 29.

7   Gyatso, *The Four Noble Truths*, 53.

8   Rahula, Walpola, *What the Buddha Taught*, (Oxford: Oneworld Publications, 1959), 18.

9   *Appropriated* here in that the innate sense of self-grasping, in leaping to the next rebirth, takes on—or appropriates—a new set of aggregates.

10 For a detailed explanation see: Tsongkhapa, *Great Treatise on the Stages of the Path to Enlightenment (Vol. 1)*, trans. Lamrim Chenmo Translation Team, (Ithaca, NY: Snow Lion Publications, 2000), 265–80.

11 Chandrakirti, *Introduction to the Middle Way*, 6:126 (translated from the Tibetan).

12 from Wangyal, Geshe, *The Door of Liberation*, (Boston: Wisdom Publications, 1973), 136.

13 The six general sufferings of samsara are: the fault of uncertainty, the fault of insatiability, the fault of casting away bodies repeatedly, the fault of repeated rebirth, the fault of repeatedly descending from high to low, and the fault of having no companions.

14 Rahula, *What the Buddha Taught*, 29.

15 Gyatso, *The Four Noble Truths*, 72.

16 Sumedho, Venerable Ajahn. *The Four Noble Truths*, (UK: Amaravati Publications, 1992), 30.

17 Sumedho, *The Four Noble Truths*, 30.

18 One of the four major Buddhist philosophical schools, the Chittamatra or Mind-only school, asserts that there are eight consciousnesses, the eighth of which, the *mind basis of all*, is just the base for karmic imprints.

19 Rahula, *What the Buddha Taught*, 31.

20 Rahula, *What the Buddha Taught*, 35.

21 Gyatso, *The Four Noble Truths*, 96.

22 Rahula, *What the Buddha Taught*, 40.

23 Gyatso, *The Four Noble Truths*, 124.

24 Rahula, *What the Buddha Taught*, 45.

25 Gyatso, *The Four Noble Truths*, 115.

26 Illustration reproduced by kind permission of Robert Beer. Taken from Beer, Robert, *The Encyclopedia of Tibetan Symbols and Motifs*. (Boston, Shambhala, 1999.), 186. Notice in this wheel the four *yin-yang* shaped sections in the center, common to many dharmachakras, that represent the four noble truths.

Glossary

ABHIDHARMA (Skt.): one of the three "baskets" of teachings from the sutras, relating to metaphysics.

AFFLICTIVE EMOTION (Skt. *klesha*): the minds caused by the fundamental confusion about how things and events exist; the second level of confusion that disturbs our minds and causes suffering.

ARHAT (Skt.): a practitioner who has achieved the state of no more learning according to the individual liberation vehicle.

ARYA (Skt.): a "superior" being, or one who has gained a direct realization of emptiness.

AVIDYA (Skt.): ignorance, which is generally divided into two types: ignorance of causality and ignorance of ultimate nature.

BODHICHITTA (Skt.): the mind that spontaneously wishes to attain enlightenment in order to benefit others; the fully open and dedicated heart.

BODHISATTVA (Skt.): someone whose spiritual practice is directed toward the achievement of enlightenment for the welfare of all beings; one who possesses the compassionate motive of bodhichitta.

BODHISATTVAYANA (Skt.): the "vehicle" of the bodhisattva, or the bodhisattva's path.

BUDDHA, a (Skt.): a fully enlightened being; one who has removed all obscurations veiling the mind and developed all good qualities to perfection; the first of the Three Jewels of refuge.

BUDDHA, the (Skt.): the historical Buddha, Shakyamuni Buddha.

BUDDHADHARMA (Skt.): the Buddha's teachings.

BUDDHAHOOD: the state of being a buddha; full enlightenment.

CONDITIONED LIFE: unenlightened existence; the state of continually being subject to the "condition" or control of other phenomena or events.

CYCLIC EXISTENCE. *See* samsara.

DESIRE REALM: of the three realms of existence within samsara, the one we live in, which is dominated by the senses. The others are the form and formless realms.

DHARMA (Skt.): literally "that which holds (one back from suffering)"; often refers to the Buddha's teachings, but more generally to anything that helps the practitioner attain liberation; the second of the Three Jewels of refuge.

DHARMAKAYA (Skt.): truth body; along with the rupakaya, one of the two bodies achieved when a being attains enlightenment; this is the result of the wisdom aspect of practice.

DHYANI BUDDHAS, THE FIVE: the five buddha families, representing five primordial energies: Vairochana, Amitabha, Akshobhya, Ratnasambhava, and Amogasiddhi.

DUKKHA (Pali): suffering, sometimes translated as "dissatisfaction."

ETERNALISM: the belief that things and events exist intrinsically; one of the two extremes to be avoided. The other extreme is nihilism.

FIVE AGGREGATES, THE: the traditional way to break down a person into psychophysical components. The aggregates are form (body), feeling, discrimination, compositional factors, and consciousness (mind).

FIVE PATHS, THE: the stages a practitioner passes through on the journey to enlightenment. They are the paths of preparation, accumulation, seeing, meditation, and no more learning.

FORM REALM: one of samsara's three realms, where beings have attained a high degree of concentration and are free from domination of the senses.

FORMLESS REALM: within samsara, the highest of the three realms, where beings have perfect concentration and have only the four mental aggregates and no physical form.

GELUG (Tib.): founded by Lama Tsongkhapa, this is one of the four schools of Tibetan Buddhism; the others are Sakya, Nyingma, and Kagyu.

INDIVIDUAL LIBERATION PRACTITIONER: a practitioner on the path to liberation (as opposed to the universal vehicle practitioner, who is on the path to enlightenment).

KARMA (Skt.): action; the natural law of cause and effect whereby positive actions produce happiness and negative actions produce suffering.

KARMIC IMPRINT (Tib. *pak chak*): the energy or propensity left by a mental act on the mindstream that will remain until it either ripens into a result or is purified.

KLESHA (Skt.): delusions—the combination of ignorance and the afflictive emotions of attachment and aversion.

LAMA TSONGKHAPA (1357–1419): a great Tibetan teacher and founder of the Gelug tradition.

LAMRIM (Tib.): the graduated path to enlightenment—the traditional presentation of the Buddha's teachings according to the Gelug school of Tibetan Buddhism.

LAMRIM CHENMO (Tib.): *The Great Stages of the Path*; the extensive lamrim text written by Lama Tsongkhapa.

MADHYAMAKA (Skt.): the middle way; the highest of the four Indian philosophical schools that are studied in Tibetan monasteries.

MAHAYANA (Skt.): literally, the Great Vehicle; representing one of the two main divisions of Buddhist thought; Mahayana is practiced in Tibet, Mongolia, China, Vietnam, Korea, and Japan; the emphasis of Mahayana thought is on bodhichitta, on the wisdom that realizes emptiness, and on enlightenment.

MERELY LABELED: phenomena's ultimate mode of existence according to the Prasangika Madhyamaka school—things are empty of inherent existence, and "merely labeled" upon a basis of designation.

MIND BASIS OF ALL: the consciousness posited by the Chittamatra (Mind Only) school to describe where the karmic imprints reside. This mind is refuted by other schools.

MOKSHA (Skt.): liberation.

NIHILISM: the extreme belief that nothing actually exists. The other extreme is eternalism.

NIRMANAKAYA (Skt.): emanation body; of the two aspects of the form body (rupakaya) of a buddha, the one that can be seen by ordinary beings.

NIRVANA (Skt.): a state of freedom from all delusions and karma, having liberated oneself from cyclic existence (samsara).

OTHER-POWERED: referring to the fact that all phenomena come into existence depending on causes and conditions—by the power of other things.

PALI: the ancient Indian language used in the earlier (Theravada) Buddhist canonical texts.

PARINIRVANA (Skt.): the state the Buddha achieved at death.

PRASANGIKA / PRASANGIKA MADHYAMAKA (Skt.): the higher of the two subdivisions of Madhyamaka school, as opposed to the Svatantrika Madhyamaka.

PRATIMOKSHA VOWS: the fundamental vows of ethical conduct taken by a spiritual practitioner, and a required preliminary for the other two sets of vows (bodhisattva and tantric) taken in highest yoga tantra initiations.

RUPAKAYA (Skt.): form body; one of the two bodies a buddha gains upon attaining enlightenment (the other is the dharmakaya); the result of the method aspect of the path.

SAMBHOGAKAYA (Skt.): enjoyment body; of the two aspects of the form body (rupakaya) of a buddha, the one that can be seen only by arya beings.

SAMSARA (Skt.): cyclic existence, the state of constantly taking rebirth due to delusions and karma.

SANSKRIT: the ancient Indian language used in Mahayana texts.

SENTIENT BEINGS: beings with sentience, i.e., any being with a mind and hence a wish to be happy and avoid suffering.

SHAMATA (Skt.): meditation for developing single-pointed concentration (samadhi).

SHASTRA (Skt.): a classical Indian commentary on the teachings of the Buddha.

SUTRA (Skt.): an actual discourse of the Buddha.

SUTRAYANA (Skt.): the vehicle of the Mahayana that takes the Buddhist sutras as their main textual source.

TANHA (Pali): thirst; the fundamental confusion that keeps us in samsara, according to the Theravada tradition.

TANTRA (Skt.): literally, thread or continuity; a text of the esoteric teachings of Buddhism; often refers to these teachings themselves.

TATAGATHA (Skt.): epithet for a buddha—literally "one thus gone."

THERAVADA (Skt.): one of the schools of early Buddhist thought; the emphasis of Theravada thought is on liberation, rather than enlightenment; the name more commonly used in Tibetan texts, Hinayana (lesser vehicle), carries an inaccurate connotation of inferiority.

THREE POISONS, THE: ignorance, aversion, and attachment—the three main mindstates that keep us in samsara—from which all other afflictive emotions arise.

TWO OBSCURATIONS, THE: the two kinds of minds that block our spiritual progress; the *obscurations of defilements*, which block us from emotional development, and the *obscurations of knowledge*, which block us from logical development, particularly the understanding of emptiness.

UNIVERSAL VEHICLE. *See* Mahayana.

BIBLIOGRAPHY

Beer, Robert. *Encyclopedia of Tibetan Symbols and Motifs*. Boston: Shambala Publications, 1999.

Bodhi, Bhikkhu, trans. *Connected Discourses of the Buddha*. Boston: Wisdom Publications, 2000.

Carus, Paul, ed. *The Gospel of Buddha*. UK: Alcove Press Ltd, 1974. First published 1915 by The Open Court Publishing Company.

The Dhammapada: The Path to Perfection. Trans. from the Pali by Juan Mascaró. UK: Penguin Books Ltd, 1973.

Gyatso, Lobsang. *The Four Noble Truths*. New York, Snow Lion Publications, 1994.

Gyatso, Tenzin, the Fourteenth Dalai Lama. *Ancient Wisdom, Modern World: Ethics for the New Millennium*. UK: Little, Brown and Co., 1999.

Gyatso, Tenzin, the Fourteenth Dalai Lama. *The Four Noble Truths*. Trans. by Thupten Jinpa, ed. by Dominique Side. London: Thorsons, 1997.

Holmes, Ken and Katia. *The Changeless Nature: A Translation of Maitreya's Uttaratantra*. Eskdalemuir, UK: Karma Drubgyud Darjay Ling, 1985.

Rahula, Walpola. *What the Buddha Taught*. Oxford: Oneworld Publications, 1959.

Sumedho, Ven. Ajhan. *The Four Noble Truths*. UK: Amaravati Publications, 1992.

Tsongkhapa, *Great Treatise on the Stages of the Path to Enlightenment (Vols. 1–3)*. Trans. Lamrim Chenmo Translation Committee. Ithaca, NY: Snow Lion Publications, 2000–2004.

Tsongkhapa and Dhargyey, Geshe Ngawang, *Lines of Experience.* Dharamsala, India: Library of Tibetan Works and Archives, 1973.

Wangyal, Geshe, *The Door of Liberation.* Boston: Wisdom Publications, 1995 (1973).

INDEX

About the Authors

Khen Rinpoche Geshe Tashi Tsering was born in Purang, West Tibet, in 1958. He and his family fled Tibet a year later, and after moving to a refugee settlement with them in Karnataka in South India, he entered Sera Mey Monastic University in 1970, graduating sixteen years later as a *lharampa geshe*, the highest level. He then studied at Gyuto Tantric monastery from 1990. Requested by Lama Thubten Zopa Rinpoche, the spiritual director of the Foundation for the Preservation of the Mahayana Tradition (FPMT), to teach in the West, he became the resident teacher at Jamyang Buddhist Centre in London in 1994, where he developed the *Foundation of Buddhist Thought* and wrote the six-volume series published by Wisdom Publications. He gained an MA in social anthropology at the School of Oriental and African Studies of London University in 2017. He has often taught in the UK, Europe, the USA, and Asia. In May 2018 Geshe Tashi was appointed the ninety-first abbot of Sera Mey Monastic University by His Holiness the Dalai Lama.

 GORDON McDOUGALL first met Tibetan Buddhism in Hong Kong in 1986, where he was the director of Cham Tse Ling, the FPMT center there, for two years. He was spiritual program coordinator of Jamyang Buddhist Centre, London, from 2000 to 2007, working with Geshe Tashi Tsering to develop the *Foundation of Buddhist Thought*. He has also led lamrim courses in the UK, Europe, and India. Since 2008 he has been editing Lama Zopa Rinpoche's teachings for Lama Yeshe Wisdom Archive and Wisdom Publications.

The Foundation of Buddhist Thought

The Foundation of Buddhist Thought is a two-year course in Buddhist studies, created by Geshe Tashi Tsering of Jamyang Buddhist Centre in London, that draws upon the depth of Tibetan Buddhist philosophy to exemplify a more realistic approach to living according to the principles of Buddhist thought. The course consists of the following six four-month modules:

> The Four Noble Truths
> Relative Truth, Ultimate Truth
> Buddhist Psychology
> The Awakening Mind
> Emptiness
> Tantra

A vital aspect of the course is Geshe Tashi's emphasis on the way these topics affect everyday life. A mixture of reading, listening, meditating, discussing, and writing ensures that each student will gain an understanding and mastery of these profound and important concepts.

To find out more about *The Foundation of Buddhist Thought*, please visit our website at buddhistthought.org. To find out more about FPMT study programs, please visit fpmt.org.

Also Available from
The Foundation of Buddhist Thought Series

"Geshi Tashi's insights can be enjoyed by a wide audience of
both specialists and newcomers to the Buddhist tradition."
THUBTEN JINPA, *principal translator for the Dalai Lama
and director of the Institute of Tibetan Classics*

RELATIVE TRUTH, ULTIMATE TRUTH
The Foundation of Buddhist Thought, Volume 2

This volume is an excellent source of support for anyone interested in cultivating
a more holistic and transformative understanding of the world around them and
ultimately of their own consciousness.

BUDDHIST PSYCHOLOGY
The Foundation of Buddhist Thought, Volume 3

Buddhist Psychology addresses both the nature of the mind and how we know what
we know. Just as scientists observe and catalog the material world, Buddhists for
centuries have been observing and cataloging the components of inner experience.

THE AWAKENING MIND
The Foundation of Buddhist Thought, Volume 4

Geshe Tashi Tsering guides students to a thorough understanding of two of the
most important methods for developing bodhichitta that have been passed down
by the great Indian and Tibetan masters over the centuries: the seven points of
cause and effect, and equalizing and exchanging the self with others.

EMPTINESS
The Foundation of Buddhist Thought, Volume 5

An incredibly welcoming presentation of the central philosophical teaching of
Mahayana Buddhism. Emptiness does not imply a nihilistic worldview, but rather
the idea that a permanent entity does not exist in any single phenomenon or
being.

TANTRA
The Foundation of Buddhist Thought, Volume 6

Anticipating the many questions Westerners have upon first encountering tantra's
colorful imagery and veiled language, *Tantra* uses straight talk to explain deities,
initiations, mandalas, and the body's subtle physiology of channels and chakras.

About Wisdom Publications

Wisdom Publications is the leading publisher of classic and contemporary Buddhist books and practical works on mindfulness. To learn more about us or to explore our other books, please visit our website at wisdomexperience.org or contact us at the address below.

Wisdom Publications
199 Elm Street
Somerville, MA 02144 USA

We are a 501(c)(3) organization, and donations in support of our mission are tax deductible.

Wisdom Publications is affiliated with the Foundation for the Preservation of the Mahayana Tradition (FPMT).